SONS AND DAUGHTERS OF THE BUDDHA

SONS AND DAUGHTERS OF THE BUDDHA

Daily Meditations from the Buddhist Tradition

Christopher Titmuss

RIDER

LONDON · SYDNEY · AUCKLAND · JOHANNESBURG

1 3 5 7 9 10 8 6 4 2

Copyright © Christopher Titmuss 2002

First published in 2002 by Rider,
an imprint of Ebury Press, Random House,
20 Vauxhall Bridge Road, London SW1V 2SA

Random House Australia (Pty) Limited
20 Alfred Street, Milsons Point, Sydney,
New South Wales 2061, Australia

Random House New Zealand Limited
18 Poland Road, Glenfield,
Auckland 10, New Zealand

Random House South Africa (Pty) Limited
Endulini, 5A Jubilee Road,
Parktown 2193, South Africa

The Random House Group Limited Reg. No. 954009

Papers used by Rider are natural, recyclable products
made from wood grown in sustainable forests.

Printed and bound by Mackays of Chatham plc, Chatham, Kent

A CIP catalogue record for this book
is available from the British Library

ISBN 0-7126-5699-5

Contents

Acknowledgements

I looked into hundreds of Buddhist books, old and new, to select a quote for each day of the year. I used the resources of the libraries at Gaia House retreat centre and Sharpham House, both in South Devon, as well as Arcturus bookshop in Totnes and the books on the bookshelves of the Buddhist Publication Group, Totnes. I also examined my own collection of Buddhist books at my Totnes home.

I spent many hours sitting in the Barrel Coffee House in Totnes with three or four books, enjoying a caffè latte. While there I would carefully look through the pages of each book until my eye fell on a worthwhile passage. I have often used two or three quotes from a particular book that I liked. I endeavoured as much as possible to take quotes that reflected an essential teaching of the author, or I picked out a quote simply because the significance of it struck me.

I wish to thank my teachers, Venerable Ajahn Dhammadharo of Supanburi, Thailand and the late Venerable Ajahn Buddhadasa of Chai Ya, Thailand. I regard both teachers as expressing the cutting edge of the Dharma (teachings of the Buddha). They are two of the finest representatives of the Buddhist Tradition: both had little time for religious ceremonies, chanting and rituals; both emphasised the importance of insight into the nature of things; and both teachers remained controversial for their bare bones approach to realisation.

I wish to express my gratitude to my daughter, Nshorna Titmuss, who kindly typed in all of the quotes. She has listed the page number of the book as well so that readers can locate the passage that I used. Thank you to the editors of Rider Books, to Jill Greenway and Susan Lascelles for their attention to detail in editing this book, and to various Dharma friends who suggested quotes to use from the Buddhist tradition.

May all beings live with compassion
May all beings live with wisdom
May all beings be enlightened

From a Son of the Buddhist Tradition

The Buddhist tradition has two faces – the outer and the inner. For any in-depth understanding of this vast, complex, decentralised and somewhat anarchic tradition, the discerning reader needs to be able distinguish one from the other to stand any chance of getting to the heart of the teachings. Like any other religion Buddhism has a public face, which is revealed in countless temples, monasteries, rituals, ceremonies and beliefs along with the endless use of flowers, candles and incense. Millions of Buddhists keep alive the outer face of Buddhism through their acts of devotion, offerings and service in order to sustain Buddhism in the world.

The Outer Face of Buddhism

The outer face of Buddhism is found not only in the Buddhist countries of Asia but also in the Asian and Western Buddhist communities, particularly in Australasia, Europe and North America. There are more temples and monasteries appearing every year in the West. Asian and Western monks and nuns take up residence in the West, working diligently to preserve the variety of forms of the Buddhist tradition, while making them available to people in the West in search of spiritual values.

The outer face of Buddhism contains a broad set of beliefs that inspire devotees to follow their particular tradition's core features. One of the strongly uniting features is belief in rebirth, namely that this existence has been shaped by past existences and serves as the catalyst for the next existence. This long-standing core belief influences the actions of body, speech and mind of countless numbers of Buddhists. It inspires them to make merit, keep precepts such as not killing and not stealing, and to make expression of devotion to the Buddha, the Dharma (the teachings of the Buddha) and the Sangha (the Order of Noble Monks and Nuns) for support.

The strong belief in the value of wholesome actions becomes the guiding force of lives of millions of Buddhists adhering to the basic tenets of the tradition, regardless of culture and region. Not surprisingly, with such value placed on meritorious behaviour, expressions of loving kindness and other forms of human goodness attract people of other backgrounds and cultures, who find themselves appreciative of contact with kindly Buddhists.

In the rural regions of Buddhist countries, local people often reveal through their manner their commitment to a wholesome life: happy, kind, smiling and polite. We tend to think of such Buddhists along these lines. It is often such a meeting with people in Buddhist countries that generates the initial interest in the teachings and practices of the Buddha.

My first visit to rural Thailand in January 1968 had a profound influence on me. I loved being in the company of Buddhist monks, nuns and laypeople. I sat down with my first teacher, Venerable Ajahn Buddhadasa, the Abbot of Wat Suanmoke (The Monastery of the Garden of Liberation) to talk about the deep things of life with him in a forest, where he spent more than fifty years. I, a 24-year-old hitch-hiker, had travelled across Europe and Asia. This enlightened master treated my countless questions seriously, and occasionally with a little amusement. It was a magical and transformative time for me. I had travelled through around thirty countries but I knew I had to make the inner journey. The Buddhist tradition pointed the way.

The Inner Face of Buddhism

The inner face of Buddhism is far more significant, as it points directly to insight, realisation and enlightenment. In the inner face of the Buddhist tradition, we look into the mind, uncover its depths and open the heart. Teachings and practices to awaken our existence belong to the inner face of Buddhism. Some teachers, including myself, have dispensed altogether with the outer face of the tradition, while others still give support to the external forms and beliefs. It is important for the discerning reader to be able to distinguish between these two faces of Buddhism. *Sons and Daughters of the Buddha* reveals the inner face of Buddhism through a wealth of insights expressed over the past 2500 years.

The religion of Buddhism is regarded as the religion of the thoughtful person. We are now witnessing in the West a period of tremendous growth of interest in the Buddha's teachings. However, to appreciate meaningful developments in the Buddhist tradition, we need first to turn our attention to the Buddha, himself.

If we look back 2500 years, the teachings of the Buddha clearly had a very radical edge. He dispensed with the caste system, animal sacrifice, rights and rituals in the texts of the Vedas. He encouraged women to go into a homeless spiritual life, abandoned all concern with the gods and goddesses that pervaded religious teachings at that time, and made liberation and enlightenment the core features of the spiritual life. He made his students look into every area of their life rather than simply adhere to a range of religious beliefs.

The Buddha also took a radically different view of his relationship to spiritual life from that of his peers. The Buddha did not claim to be God, nor the Son of God, nor a prophet, nor an agent of God, nor did he reduce himself to the level of an ordinary mortal struggling to get through existence as peacefully as possible. When asked about himself, the Buddha said, 'I am awake.'

Some might perceive such a remark as arrogant or, at least, as demonstrating a need to impress others, but we can see from the texts that he regarded his awakening to the nature of things as a simple statement of fact. It meant for him that the world of change, of problems and misfortunes had ceased to have any grip whatsoever over his consciousness. He had seen through the countless myths that uphold our existence, and had shaken off the layers of armour that uphold the self. The Buddha had woken up to things as they really are.

The Buddha's presence, his extraordinary depth of insight and his deep feelings of concern for the well-being of others inspired huge numbers of people to listen to his teachings and follow his instructions on spiritual practice. He dispensed with the 'guru' role of spiritual teachers, and instead referred to himself as a 'good friend' living the same very basic lifestyle as his students.

The spirit for such enquiry into existence has sustained itself through twenty-five centuries. These creative and insightful teachings stretched as far as Afghanistan in the west of Asia, to Sri Lanka in southern Asia and to the far north of Japan and China. As the Dharma took root in these regions, it gave birth to a variety of traditions, including Theravada, Mahayana, Tantra, Vajrayana, Zen, Chaan and Pure Land etc. Numerous books on Buddhism offer descriptions of the basic similarities and differences between these traditions.

Within these major traditions, there are numerous smaller traditions and lineages. One teacher may give rise to several different types of traditions, as different students who become teachers adapt their understanding of their teacher's message. For the beginner, it can be hard to make sense of it. I have spent my adult life connected with the Buddhist tradition, and there is still a certain mystery to the web of it all.

The teachings and practices adapted themselves to the culture and environment of the region; sometimes including breathtaking differences in the emphasis of the teachings from one region to another or in the same region. Some teachers emphasise form, ritual, method, technique and guru devotion, while other teachers dismiss form, ritual, method, technique and guru devotion. Venerable Ajahn Buddhadasa, the leading reformer of Theravada Buddhism in the twentieth century, described lighting of candles and offering flowers at the altar for the Buddha in temples as 'Buddhism for thumbsucking kids'. The real heart of the teachings lies in the depth of insight and wisdom. Nowhere else.

What we experience today is the gradual assimilation of the Buddhist tradition into Western society. The tradition offers fresh perspectives on spiritual wisdom. There is a desperate vacuum in Western society, where the primary reason for existence has become the sole pursuit of the interests of the self. It has led to a society mercilessly trapped in the extremes of self-interest or self-hatred, unable to look at daily life in any other way.

The Buddhist tradition challenges the whole construction of the self, its likes and dislikes, the forces of desire and rejection and the endless number of conflicts burning up within or involving other people. It is not an easy undertaking but a remarkable enquiry to find out other ways of perceiving daily life. If we are quietly determined to cut through the outer face of Buddhism to reach what the teachers of this tradition are pointing out, then we too will be on the cutting edge of a remarkable tradition; for it is a tradition that lives and dies on the strengths of its insights and its ability to transform the lives of men, women and children.

There is no God, no Saviour, no sacred book to believe in, nor anybody to espouse a divine word or revelation. The tradition has taken no interest in such hyperbole that gives special authority to what is said or written through wrapping it up in religious significance.

For a number of readers, some of the Buddhist teachers referred to in this collection of 365 quotes will already be familiar. You will have read some of their books and understand the emphasis in their particular teaching. Other readers will hardly recognise a single name from the variety of teachers that are quoted. From the standpoint of the tradition, the name and personal history of the teacher matters little, whereas what the teacher has written matters very much. This is the right priority.

The Buddhist tradition has engaged in a long-standing exploration of the inner life including the way perceptions and feelings become thoughts, and thoughts become words expressed out in the world, both orally and in written form. When do a group of words become an insight for the reader? It is hard to comprehend what constitutes an insight. We might say there is a certain congruence of the inner life with what is on paper. Time and place are supportive conditions. We may read with one mind-set and the words fall like seeds on hard rock. We can read the same thing later and every sentence becomes a jewel, utterly relevant to us in that particular moment. There is much to be said for reading the same quote on different occasions, so that it has the opportunity to strike home. The insight matters more than the content of the words on paper.

The primary intention behind putting the book together is to encourage readers to develop an awareness that allows some deep truths of life to register, thus opening the mind to a different dimension of things. In a culture where success becomes determined by wealth and ownership, society is in desperate need of finding ways to turn the mind around to another kind of vision. The quotes in this book reflect a diversity of concerns and insights that will challenge your countless assumptions about life.

If you are a Buddhist, you will be familiar with the investigation into suffering, desire impermanence, letting go, tolerance, compassion, meditation, wisdom, inter-connection, emptiness of 'I' and 'my', liberation and enlightenment. These themes run through the Buddhist worldview. Inspired by the Buddha, the tradition gives sympathetic support to the plight of people, animals and the environment. What is the heart of the message of the Buddha and the Buddhist tradition? It is best summarised in two words: 'Wake Up!'

Sons and Daughters of the Buddha follows in the footsteps of the Buddha through attempting to point out unshakeable truths of existence, even when they are uncomfortable to hear. If we do not wake up, we will sleep-walk through life remaining completely obsessed with our fantasies, personal needs and relentless expectations of others and ourselves. If we wake up we will put an end to living in a realm of self-created myths that haunt our daily life, bringing distress or the conceited self-delusion that we think we live in the real world.

No doubt, some of the quotes will strike a real cord with some of the readers. Your first thought may be the wish to rush out and purchase a copy of that particular book which contains the quote. That may be worthwhile but it may not be necessary. That single quote may carry more weight in your life than all of the rest of the book put together.

Let us not underestimate the extraordinary potency of a few lines. In the old days Buddhist monks and nuns went to the cave or jungle armed with only a few verses. Their teachers made it clear to them that a single verse has more potential to wake them up than memorising the thousands of talks that the Buddha gave. During my six years as a Buddhist monk in Thailand and India, I spent about nine months in solitude in a cave. I took with me a small book called *Woven Cadences* (*Sutta Nipata, Verses of the Buddha* translated by E.M. Hare) to meditate on the two short closing chapters of verses of the Buddha. It was more than enough reading for that period of time.

Have confidence in the quote that you read. It is not particularly important what came before the text nor what comes after it. The meditation for 22 April consists of a blank page to indicate the inability of words to express the inexpressible. I have intentionally selected a number of quotes far too deep for the ordinary mind to be able to comprehend. The deepest understanding has to come from a place beyond our conventional mental faculties. The great teachers of the Buddhist tradition have spoken from 'The Beyond' to remind students of the conventionality of many of their perceptions and understanding. The mind, with all of its accumulated knowledge and experience, has to give up on itself, on its efforts to try to work out the meaning of an abiding truth.

In Buddhist terms, it is liberating to see the emptiness of the mind as a vehicle for the deepest level of insights about the nature of things. As you read *Sons and Daughters of the Buddha,* you will come across some gems entirely suited to your existence. The words will speak directly to you, to your awakening, to your Buddha mind. Those quotes are the important ones. Absorb them. Reflect on them. Meditate on them. These quotes will provide a foundation for wisdom, acting in the same way as a very good friend in time of need. You have in your hands a remarkable resource. The tradition has pointed out that we know the taste of pure water only through drinking it.

Christopher Titmuss
Totnes
Devon
England

From a Daughter of the
Buddhist Tradition

I experienced the Buddhist tradition from an early age. Six months after I was born in the summer of 1981, my parents, Christopher Titmuss and Gwanwyn Williams, took me to India to visit Bodh Gaya, the place of the Buddha's enlightenment, and Sarnath, where the Buddha gave his first teachings. This early experience proved to be the foundation for my contact with Buddhism. Since then I have travelled with my father to various Buddhist centres in four continents.

Buddhism is a beautiful religion. Having been exposed to it through my father, I can confidently say Buddhism is a religion that you can devote your life to or simply benefit from the insights it offers. This book caters for both types of commitment.

My father spent many, many hours reading and selecting quotes from a wide variety of Buddhists books. I then typed up the 365 high-lighted quotes, leaving the result that you have in front of you. Whilst working on this project I was able to read, type and absorb the text I was entering. I realised it was helpful for me to read some quotes several times or read them out aloud. This ensured a possibility for appreciation of the message that was being portrayed. The overall contents of the quotes communicated to me that the core of these teachings is wisdom. When you have read the quotes, I am sure you will draw the same conclusion. The main task of the Buddhist tradition points to realising wisdom in the presence of life.

Do you frequently awake in the morning with lack of motivation and little sense of what the forthcoming day will hold for you? Or do you rise with a burst of enthusiasm, itching to face the challenges that will cross your path for that day? In either case, directly absorbing a quote could prove invaluable to the way in which your day turns out. *Sons and Daughters of the Buddha* gives you the opportunity of benefiting your daily life through reflecting on a daily quote to incorporate into everyday situations.

Although I would not consider myself a member of any particular religion, I feel I can extract practices and teachings from different faiths which correspond with my vision of a worthwhile life. The purpose of this book is to provide a broad understanding of Buddhist Tradition, not to convert or preach various beliefs.

These quotations also provide an opportunity to develop a useful daily spiritual discipline. Put aside a few moments of each day to read and reflect on your quote for the day. Some are deep and often hard to comprehend initially, others are light, even humorous, but they all have the ability to benefit you and those people you interact with on that day.

I have enjoyed entering the quotes. I hope all the efforts to put this book together will bring love and wisdom to your daily life.

Nshorna Titmuss,
Torquay
Devon
England

SONS AND DAUGHTERS OF THE BUDDHA

JANUARY 1

Nothing whatsoever should be clung to as 'I' or 'mine'.

JANUARY 2

✳

Because we all share this small planet earth, we have to learn to live in harmony and peace with each other and with nature. This is not just a dream, but a necessity. We are dependent on each other in so many ways that we can no longer live in isolated communities and ignore what is happening outside those communities. We need to help each other when we have difficulties, and we must share the good fortune that we enjoy. I speak to you as just another human being, as a simple monk. If you find what I say useful, then I hope you will try to put it into practice.

JANUARY 3

A light does not need to think, 'I am dispelling darkness' – it simply illuminates. Awareness is an inner light that enables us to see things more clearly. It dispels the heaviness of how things appear to us, thus weakening our clinging or aversion to them.

JANUARY 4

✳

When others, out of jealousy,
Mistreat me with abuse, slander and scorn,
I will practise accepting defeat
And offering victory to them.

JANUARY 5

❄

Repressed sensuality may break through in day-dreams and fantasy, and give them their force and compulsiveness. A person acts out in fantasy what he does not dare to put into actual effect, owing to his inhibition. If one looks for what is common to all these fantasies, the insight gained into unconscious driving forces and compensations may cut the ground from under them.

JANUARY 6

To live abroad for a time may at least help one to see the relative nature of one's customs and habits. National pride, which some consider as the most stupid sort of pride, falls into this category.

JANUARY 7

✳

There is a famous parable in the *Republic* of Plato about a cave. In the cave is a row of people, chained in such a way that they can only face the back wall. Behind the row of people, is a fire and a procession of figures walking by engaged in the activities of life. The procession of figures casts shadows on the back wall of the cave. The people who are chained can see only the changing view of shadows, and because that is all they have ever seen, they take these shadows to be ultimate reality.

Sometimes a person who is bound in this way, through great effort, manages to loosen the chains and turn around. He or she sees the fire and procession and begins to understand that the shadows are not the reality, but merely a reflection on the wall. Perhaps with further effort that person is able to cut the chains completely and emerge into the sunlight, into freedom.

JANUARY 8

The practice of giving is universally recognised as one of the most basic human virtues, a quality that testifies to the depth of one's humanity and one's capacity for self-transcendence. In the teachings of the Buddha, too, the practice of giving claims a place of special eminence, one which singles it out as being in a sense the foundation and seed of spiritual development.

JANUARY 9

Personal help and example are still essential and may be all we can give, but they will fall short of fully effective helping. This requires working to change the social institutions and structures which affirm coerciveness and indifference and maintain their karmic momentum. Again, it is the Buddhist recognition of the power of conditioning – which points up the importance of a radical and transformative social activism.

JANUARY 10

❋

The Father and Mother Buddha are my parents
The immaculate Dharma is my face
The assembly of Sangha are my cousins and nephews
And the guardians of Dharma are my friends.
These four are my lasting heavenly kinsmen.
Your worldly kinsmen are deceitful and delusive
Without hesitation, I throw all ephemeral associates away.

JANUARY 11

❋

Chao-chou: What is the way?

Master Nan-chi'uuan: Ordinary mind is the way.

Chao-chou: How should I pursue it?

Master Nan-ch'uuan: If you move towards it, it moves away.

JANUARY 12

The known object and the knowing mind are all in a state of flux, now appearing, now vanishing. They are transitory. There is no essence or substance worthy to be named 'mine' in them. They signify only the process of becoming and dissolution.

JANUARY 13

Watch a flash of lightning. If you watch it at the moment lightning strikes, you will see it for yourself. If you are imagining in your mind how lightning strikes before or after the event, you may not be regarded as having seen the flash of lightning. So try to know things for yourself by actual observation of things as they happen.

JANUARY 14

Manjusri: What is the root of good and evil?

Vimalakirti: Materiality is the root of good and evil.

Manjusri: What is the root of materiality?

Vimalakirti: Desire is the root of materiality.

Manjusri: What is the root of desire and attachment?

Vimalakirti: Unreal construction is the root of desire.

Manjusri: What is the root of unreal construction?

Vimalakirti: The false concept is its root.

Manjusri: What is the root of the false concept?

Vimalakirti: Baselessness.

Manjusri: What is the root of baselessness?

Vimalakirti: Manjusri, when something is baseless, how can it have any root? Therefore, all things stand on the root which is baseless.

JANUARY 15

Manjusri: to know no one teaching, to express nothing, to say nothing, to explain nothing, to announce nothing, to indicate nothing – that is the entrance into non-duality.

JANUARY 16

As human brothers and sisters, I have a feeling that deep down we are all the same human beings. Therefore it is quite natural that when some human brothers and sisters suffer, then other brothers and sisters spontaneously develop some sort of sincere feeling or concern. At this moment I find this very much alive. I consider this a hope for the future.

JANUARY 17

Learning to distinguish wisdom from dependence can be aided by understanding our own early history. We can reflect on how needs were met in our own family, how limits were set, how insecurity was treated. Until we become aware of them, we will repeat these family patterns in our spiritual life.

JANUARY 18

Zen Master:

Do not search for truth
Just stop having opinions.

JANUARY 19

'All this Zen stuff is nonsense,' said the sceptic.

'You are perfectly correct,' responded the master, 'but this is a teaching I normally reserve for my most advanced students.'

JANUARY 20

❋

Real beauty is something within, something in the mind. If the beauty of Dharma is present in a person, then that person is beautiful. That person possesses the beauty of Dharma in body, speech, and mind. It has nothing at all to do with external appearances, wealth or level of education, though a person who has superficial beauty also, is beautiful in both ways, both within and without. If you must choose between external beauty and internal beauty, which kind will you take? Think it over.

JANUARY 21

In ordinary everyday language, darkness is absence of
light, which makes it impossible to see. In Dhamma
language, darkness is lack of insight, ignorance of the
truth, spiritual blindness. This is true darkness. If a
person lacking true insight were to go and sit right in
full sunlight, that person would still be in darkness,
the darkness of ignorance as to the true nature of
things.

JANUARY 22

The root of suffering is clinging, the root of clinging is craving, and the root of craving is ignorance.

JANUARY 23

As in a dream, things that are not there appear to the deluded.
As in a magic show, things are made to appear by a temporary conjunction of causes, circumstances and connections.
As in an optical illusion, things appear to be there, yet there is nothing.
As in a mirage, things appear but are not real.
As in an echo, things can be perceived but there is nothing there, either outside or inside.

❊

These days, lamas and monks, whom one might expect to be a little better than others, and who know about the principle of cause and effect, are so afraid of the defilements attached to offerings that they refuse even to give blessings or say dedication prayers for suffering beings who are sick or dead. In so doing they cut the love and compassion of bodhicitta at the root.

The majority are extremely selfish. They take part in ceremonies at the request of their benefactors. But, instead of reciting what the families in question need, they pull out their own prayer books, grimy and worn out from long use, and with the excuse that they must not interrupt the continuity of their own personal practice, they recite from that while everyone else is reciting the prayers.

JANUARY 25

Too much adventure, romance and excitement wears you out because you get so caught in it. You're pulled along by it, and you have no way to resist or let go of it. If you have no wisdom, you just get pulled along into one rebirth after another. These rebirths – based on desire – are the ones you can witness through meditation. When you see them, you understand what rebirth is.

If you understand rebirth on the everyday level, you'll appreciate how it must operate at the time of death.

JANUARY 26

❉

Contemplate the feeling of being praised. Notice
what it does to your life when somebody says that
you're a beautiful or wonderful person. You can
observe that feeling of happiness, rather than just
being carried along in it. If somebody really hates
you and criticises you, you can be carried away with
anger or resentment or grief; but as an alternative,
you can contemplate it. You can transcend the feeling
realm by accepting and observing it, rather than being
swept away in it or judging it.

JANUARY 27

Some people unfamiliar with Buddhism, see it as a dry, joyless, spiritual path that leads to a similar kind of ground: the end of suffering. The Buddha's teachings arose in the midst of Hinduism, which saw life as intense suffering and little else, and in comparison it may have seemed that what Buddhism had to offer was at least better than a life of pain.

Yet, far from being a dry, joyless, intellectual exercise in casting off pain, the path that Buddha offered is one of turning toward and moving into joy.

❋

The moment I die,
I will try to come back to you
as quickly as possible.
I promise it will not take long.
Isn't it true
I am already with you,
as I die each moment?
I come back to you
in every moment.
Just look,
feel my presence.
If you want to cry,
please cry.
And know
that I will cry with you.
The tears you shed
will heal us both.
Your tears are mine.
The earth I tread this morning
transcends history.
Spring and winter are both present in the moment.
The young leaf and the dead leaf are really one.
My feet touch deathlessness,
and my feet are yours.
Walk with me now.

JANUARY 29

❄

We are inexorably tied to the ever-changing phenomenal world. When things move, we move with them. We are in a continual state of compelled transition. It is impossible to be the master of one's consciousness under such conditions. Of course we may think that we are our own masters but this is a fantasy. We are fooling ourselves. In reality we are constantly influenced by and reacting to outside events.

JANUARY 30

Now we turn to a rather strange word, the word *Mara* (the tempter, the devil). The *Mara* of everyday language is conceived as a kind of monster with body, face and eyes of repulsive and terrifying appearance. *Mara* in Dhamma language, however, is not a living creature but rather any kind of mental state opposed to the good and wholesome and to progress towards the cessation of *dukkha* (suffering). That which opposes and obstructs spiritual progress is called *Mara*. We may think of *Mara* as a living being if we wish, as long as we understand what he really stands for.

JANUARY 31

❉

Faith is the firm foundation of my house
Diligence forms the high walls
Meditation makes the huge bricks
And wisdom is the great cornerstone.
With these four things, I built my castle
And it will last as long as the Truth eternal.
Your worldly houses are delusions
Mere prisons for the demons,
And so I would abandon and desert them.

FEBRUARY 1

✳

Taking what is not given is of three kinds: taking by force, taking by stealth and taking by trickery.

Taking by force. Also called taking by overpowering, this means the forceful seizure of possessions or property by a powerful individual such as a king having no legal right to them. It also includes plunder by force of numbers, as by an army, for example.

Taking by stealth. This means to take possession of things secretly, like a burglar, without being seen by the owner.

Taking by trickery. This is to take others' goods, in a business deal for example, by lying to the other party, using false weights and measures or other such subterfuges.

FEBRUARY 2

When you wake up in the morning, do not suddenly jump out of bed like a cow or sheep from its pen. While you are still in bed, relax your mind; turn within and examine it carefully. If you have done anything negative during the night in your dreams, regret it and confess. On the other hand, if you have done something positive be glad and dedicate the merit to the benefit of all beings. Arouse bodhichitta, thinking: 'Today I will do whatever good I can and avoid evil as much as possible, so that all infinite beings may attain perfect Buddhahood.'

FEBRUARY 3

Ryokan's simple mountain hut was burgled one night. The thief found nothing but the master meditating. Ryokan said, 'You have come so far, I can not let you leave empty-handed. Here take the clothes I am wearing.'

The thief left very confused. The master mused, 'Poor man, I wish I could have given him this exquisite moon.'

FEBRUARY 4

❄

Two monks were arguing. One said, 'The flag is moving.' The other said, 'No, the wind is moving.' On hearing their dispute Hui-neng said, 'It is neither the flag nor the wind that is moving. It is your mind that moves.'

FEBRUARY 5

Do work of all kinds with a mind that is void.

FEBRUARY 6

Ignorant people always have attachment in one form or another to everything that is or is not. As a result, desirable things are all converted into causes of suffering. Good is also transformed into suffering. Praise, fame, honour and the like are all turned into forms of suffering as soon as you try to seize and hang on to them. All becomes unsatisfactory because of grasping and clinging, and all is suffering equally.

Whether good or evil, merit or sin, happiness or unhappiness, gain or loss; all dualistic concepts become causes of suffering whenever you are attached to one or the other.

FEBRUARY 7

A constant threat to the vitality of religion is the tendency to raise its conceptual and symbolic framework to ultimacy, and then to concern oneself only with its structural forms instead of the inner meaning to which these structural features refer. This trend, together with its destructive consequences, can be clearly seen upon a perusal of the history of most religions.

FEBRUARY 8

Equanimity sees through the superficial veneer projected upon others by desirous attachment, aversion and indifference. Under the influence of these attitudes others actually appear to us as though desirability, repugnance or insignificance were inherent characteristics of their vital essence.

FEBRUARY 9

❋

Significantly, when we do *metta* (loving kindness) practice, we begin by directing *metta* towards ourselves. This is the essential foundation for being able to offer genuine love to others. When we truly love ourselves, we want to take care of others, because that is what is most enriching or nourishing for us.

FEBRUARY 10

When we steep our hearts in loving kindness, we are able to sleep easily, and to have pleasant dreams. To have self-respect in life, to walk through this life with grace and confidence, means having a commitment to non-harming and to loving care.

FEBRUARY 11

I have seen a beggar in Calcutta, with no arms or legs, because of leprosy, crawling along the streets with a bucket in her mouth into which people dropped money. Despite her suffering, she wanted to live. I have also known people here in the United States who have had healthy bodies and financial resources, who have received care from others who love them, and yet these people have wanted to die.

FEBRUARY 12

Rather it is a law of the universe that as we give, we receive. When you know someone who is very generous, even if he or she has not given to you directly, what does it feel like as you call this person to mind? People who are generous awaken in us openness, love and delight.

FEBRUARY 13

Though righteous indignation sits on a higher pedestal, as it is directed against evil persons and evil, if not well handled, it can provide the base for more violent reactions. Unjust systems as well as morally degenerate actions have provided targets for diverse expressions of violence.

FEBRUARY 14

Limitless compassion is difficult to define but it may be compared to the strength and depth of feeling that exists between a mother and her child, being extended to all beings equally everywhere.

FEBRUARY 15

The false sense of self is the root of afflictions:
ignorance working through the false sense of self is
thus at the root of our being limited to the rounds of
birth and death, and thus at the root of all our han-
kering and suffering.

FEBRUARY 16

❄

To integrate meditation with life, the Buddhist masters tell us there is no substitute for regular practice, for only through real practice will we be able to taste unbrokenly the calm of our true nature of mind, and so be able to sustain the experience of it in our everyday life. That is why developing stability in spiritual practice is so important, through first practising in the right environment and in proper practice sessions and then mixing the experience of practice with everyday life.

Sogyal Rinpoche

FEBRUARY 17

✳

As organic expressions of life on earth, we have a long and panoramic history. We are not yesterday's child, nor limited to this one brief moment of our planet's story: our roots go back to the beginning of time. We can learn to remember them. The knowledge is in us.

FEBRUARY 18

The Buddha emphasises over and over that we are enslaved to the mind. By being attached to its contents, we are propelled into actions that cause suffering for ourselves and others. The purpose of his teaching is to free us from this attachment, to master the mind. But you don't accomplish this task by brute force. It is clear seeing that makes us true guardians of the heart.

FEBRUARY 19

In many Buddhist temples, monasteries and meditation centres, flower arrangements are part of the décor, and they not only beautify the setting but also offer a valuable teaching. On the first day the flowers are fresh and beautiful, vibrant and fragrant, and it heartens us to see them. On the second day, perhaps they have lost some of their fragrance. Soon they begin to droop, the petals start to fall and before long – despite our admiration – they go and die on us.

Do we conclude from that experience that we'll never enjoy a flower again, because they always wither and die and disappoint us? Or do we enjoy them while they're here, take them in fully when we're with them and when they're gone, experience a moment's sadness and move on? It's the same with any human experience. It's the same with rapture and happiness.

FEBRUARY 20

While you are performing a bodily act, you should reflect on it . . . . If, on reflection, you know that it led to self-affliction, to the affliction of others, or to both, it was an unskilful bodily act with painful consequences, painful results, then you should confess it, reveal it, lay it open to the teacher or to a knowledgeable companion in the holy life. Having confessed it . . . you should exercise restraint in the future. But if on reflection you know that it did not lead to affliction . . . it was a skilful bodily act with happy consequences, happy results, then you should stay mentally refreshed and joyful, training day and night in skilful mental qualities.

FEBRUARY 21

Once one has attained full awakening and needs to do nothing more for one's own welfare, one continues to act for the welfare of others.

FEBRUARY 22

Reality is nothing but what is happening right here, right now. Things just happen, just move, just change. We can't pin them down by taking a snapshot. That's what all our ideas and concepts amount to – a pile of snapshots. We just have to see this directly. That's the state of emptiness, while the snapshots constitute the world of form. And the Heart Sutra is saying, once again, that these two worlds are the same.

FEBRUARY 23

Intimacy has a very special meaning and flavour in Zen. It's an intimacy that's closely related to harmony and to the word *Kai*. The analogy of the ink spots diffused in the viscous liquid is helpful in understanding this. We speak of the intimacy of the ink and the liquid, an intimacy so intimate that we don't even see or grasp it. What is so much in front of us that we can't see it? Life as it is.

FEBRUARY 24

I arrived in the United States on 4 July 1976, the two hundredth anniversary of America's birth. The country's determination to hold on to its old image of power, might and right, had collapsed under its own weight, and by 1976, these notions had disappeared within the pain of the Vietnam War. Nothing seemed sure any more. Despite the hopeful exterior, a crack had become noticeably apparent in the centre of the collective American mind. Fear for America's future was hiding beneath the surface of the American dream.

FEBRUARY 25

A conquering tyrant and his armies were sweeping through the country, laying waste all before them. When they arrived at a certain village, all the inhabitants had taken refuge in the surrounding hills, except for one old monk. The tyrant was enraged at the impudence of the monk and personally stormed into the monastery and confronted him face to face. 'Don't you know who I am?' he bellowed at the still, quiet master. 'I could draw my sword and cut you in two and not blink an eye.'

The master smiled serenely and replied; ' Don't you know who I am? I could stand here while you draw your sword and cut me in two, and not blink an eye.'

FEBRUARY 26

On the subway yesterday, as I read the Diamond Sutra, not that, the Surangama Sutra, I realised that everybody in the subway and all their thoughts and interests and the subway itself and their poor shoes and gloves etc., and the cellophane paper on the floor and the poor dust in the corners was all of one suchness and essence.

*Extract from letter by Jack Kerouac to
Allen Ginsberg on 18 January, 1955*

FEBRUARY 27

❊

A Buddha in the Woodpile

If there had been only
one Buddhist in the woodpile
In Waco Texas
to teach us how to sit still
one saffron Budhhist in the back rooms
just one Tibetan lama
just one Taoist
just one Zen
just one Thomas Merton Trappist
just one saint in the wilderness
of Waco USA . . .
But not a glimmer got through
The security screened it out
screened out the Buddha
and his not so-scary wisdom . . .
Then that sick cult and its children
might still be breathing
the free American air
of the First Amendment.

Lawrence Ferlinghetti

FEBRUARY 28

Goodbye Heaven, farewell Nirvana, sad Paradise adieu, adios all Angels and Archangels, Devas and Devakis, Bodhisattvas, Buddhas, rings of Seraphim, Constellations of Elect Souls weeping singing in the golden Bhumi Rungs, goodbye High Throne, High Central Place, Alleluia Light beyond Light, a wave of the hand to thee central Golden Rose.

Allen Ginsberg

MARCH 1

✳

There are two types of knowledge – knowledge of the worldly realm and knowledge of the spiritual, or true wisdom. If we have not yet practised and trained ourselves, no matter how much knowledge we have, it is still worldly, and thus cannot liberate us.

MARCH 2

The Dhamma of the Buddha is not found in books. If you want to really see for yourself what the Buddha was talking about, you don't need to bother with the books. Watch your own mind. Examine to see how feelings come and go, how thoughts come and go. Don't be attached to anything. Just be mindful of whatever there is to see. This is the way to the truths of the Buddha.

MARCH 3

✳

The profound state of emptiness
Dries up the ocean of passion.
It crumples the mountain of anger.
It illuminates the darkness of stupidity.
It calms down the gale of jealousy.
It defeats the illness of the Kleshas (problems)
It is a friend in sorrow.

It subdues the demon of ego-fixation.
It turns negative conditions into aids.
It turns bad omens into good luck.
It causes to manifest complete enlightenment.
It gives birth to the Buddhas of the three times
(past, present, future).
Emptiness is the Darmakaya mother.

There is no teaching higher than emptiness.
There is no teaching swifter than emptiness.
There is no teaching more excellent than emptiness.
There is no teaching more profound than emptiness.

MARCH 4

❉

Inwardly, watch the nature of your mind,
Sky-like effortless natural mind,
Nature as it is, spontaneously pure from the very
beginning,
Absolute truth, beyond accomplishment through
effort with cause and conditions,
Great gnosis of self-luminosity, innate wakefulness,
one's own intrinsic awareness,
Transcending all the inhibitions, dwelling upon,
coming and going,
The natural state free from concepts, mental
projections and absorptions.

MARCH 5

❄

I was utterly poor, living hand to mouth on the streets in Calcutta, wandering around with my hand out begging for pennies. So many unexpected ups and downs, who can describe them? Life is like that, full of unexpected twists and turns – illusory, impermanent, ungovernable and unstable. And in the end, we all die. What a spectacle.

I unexpectedly found myself riding across vast oceans in jet planes, and coasting up and down the length of giant needle-shaped sky scrapers, in boxcarlike air-conditioned elevators in the great capitals of the modern world, sleeping in both grand hotels and on the rugs and couches of modern living rooms, eating in restaurants and outdoors on sunny patios, being served like a king.

MARCH 6

It is not difficult to see the lack of reflection present in most people in society. Even to understand the workings of things on an elementary level, such as in seeing the cause and effect involved in personal actions, is beyond most people's awareness. Most people follow the crowd. This is the way society usually operates, and this is social kamma.

MARCH 7

Zen Master Dogen has said:

> To study Buddhism is to study the self.
> To study the self is to forget the self.
> To forget the self is to be one with others.

MARCH 8

❋

I often have the experience as a therapist of helping someone discover a difficult feeling like anger and then hearing them ask, 'What do I do now? Should I go home and have it out?'

Sometimes we feel that the only solution is to act out every emotion that we get in touch with. We feel as if we must express it to whomever it is directed or that we are somehow cheating ourselves. The idea of simply knowing the feeling does not occur to us.

MARCH 9

❄

As the third Zen Patriarch, writing in the early seventh century AD, articulated with great clarity:

> When the mind exists undisturbed in the way,
> nothing in the world can offend,
> and when a thing can no longer offend,
> it ceases to exist in the old way . . .
> If you wish to move in the One way
> Do not dislike even the world of senses and ideas.
> Indeed, to accept them fully
> Is identical with true enlightenment.

Training in this attitude of mind is why meditation is practised.

MARCH 10

The Buddha said emphatically, 'This is a truth to be realised here and now.' We do not have to wait until we die to find out if it's all true – this teaching is for living human beings like ourselves. Each one of us has to realise it. I may tell you about it and encourage you to do it but I can't make you realise it!

MARCH 11

With right effort, there can be a cool kind of acceptance of a situation rather than the panic that comes from thinking that it's up to me to set everybody straight, to make everything right and solve everybody's problems. We do the best we can, but we also realise that it's not up to us to do everything and make everything right.

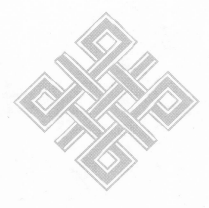

MARCH 12

✻

When acquainted with the peace of mind bestowed by the attitude of bare attention, one will be less tempted to rush into action or to interfere in other people's affairs. If, in that way, complications and conflicts of all kinds are lessened, the endeavour to shape the mind will meet with little resistance.

Bare attention is concerned only with the present. It teaches what so many have forgotten; to live with full awareness in the here and now. It teaches us to face the present without trying to escape into thoughts about the past or future.

MARCH 13

Like the fabled frog who imagined the water in his well to be unsurpassed in depth and vastness and knew not of the deep, vast ocean, world-fettered man comprehends only the small and knows nothing of the great.

MARCH 14

He who does not know that such preaching is only a skilful device may be likened to the child who picks up pebbles and calls them gems. Without effort on my part the Buddha nature manifests itself. This is due neither to the instruction of my teacher nor to any attainment of my own.

MARCH 15

If a man could eliminate suffering by making offerings, paying homage and praying, there would be no-one subject to suffering left in the world; because anyone at all can pay homage and pray. But since people are still subject to suffering while in the very act of making obeisances, paying homage and performing rights, this is clearly not the way to gain liberation.

MARCH 16

To give your sheep or cow a large spacious meadow
is the way to control him.

MARCH 17

If your mind is empty, it is always ready for anything; it is open to everything. In the beginner's mind there are many possibilities; in the expert's mind there are few.

MARCH 18

It is a kind of mystery that for people who have no experience of enlightenment, enlightenment is something wonderful. But if they attain it, it is nothing. But yet it is not nothing. Do you understand?

MARCH 19

The sky is never surprised when all of a sudden a thunderbolt breaks through.

MARCH 20

What a relief it was to refrain from adding all my stored up stories of hurtful remarks that I thought he had made about me on previous occasions. 'I like you' or 'I don't like you' is part of our neurological memory bank, very likely an instinctive safety device. It's very strong, but it's really not coming from our clearest level of understanding. Balanced attention, erasing fear and resentment, makes genuine appreciation and friendship possible.

MARCH 21

If we are to be a humane society, we must feed all the children who are hungry, clothe all the children who are cold, and care for all our children with respect, loving kindness and integrity. We must care for every child as if he or she were the Buddha.

MARCH 22

❉

The sage looked at the world
And said –
with good friends
even a fool can be wise.

Keep good company,
and wisdom grows.
Those who keep good company
can be freed from suffering.

We have to understand suffering,
the cause of suffering,
its end,
and the eightfold way –
these are the four noble truths.

So I destroy greed and hate
with a sizzle.
And I am the same woman
who goes to the foot of a tree
and says to herself,
'Ah happiness,'
and meditates with happiness.

MARCH 24

Vimala became a renunciant who is not afraid of the
world, a person who is truly free.

Young,
intoxicated by my own
Lovely skin,
my figure,
my gorgeous looks,
and famous too,
I despised other women.

Dressed to kill
at the whorehouse door,
I was a hunter
and spread my snare for fools.

And when I stripped for them
I was the woman of their dreams;
I laughed as I teased them.

Today,
head shaved,
robed,
alms-wanderer,
I, my same self,
sit at the tree's foot;
no thought.

All ties
untied,
I have cut men and gods
out of my life,

I have quenched the fires.

MARCH 25

�֎

One twelve-year-old boy, when asked by his father what he would like for his birthday, said, 'Daddy, I want you!' His father was rarely at home. He was quite wealthy but he worked all the time to provide for his family. His son was a bell of mindfulness for him. The little boy understood that the greatest gift we can offer our loved ones is our true presence.

MARCH 26

❄

We must be careful to avoid ingesting toxins in the form of violent TV programmes, video games, movies, magazines and books. When we watch that kind of violence we water our own negative seeds, our tendencies, and eventually we will think and act out of those seeds. Because of the violent toxins in so many people's minds, and in our minds too, it has become dangerous to walk alone at night in many cities. Young people stare at television sets hour after hour, and their minds are invaded by programmes selected by irresponsible producers.

MARCH 27

Peace activist A.J. Muste said 'There is no way to peace, peace is the way.' He meant that we can realise peace right in the present moment with each look, smile, word and action. Peace is not just an end. Each step we make we should be peace, should be happiness. Precepts and commandments help us dwell in peace, knowing what to do and what not to do in the present moment. They are treasures that lead us along a path of beauty, wholesomeness and truth. They contain the wisdom of our spiritual traditions and when we practise them, our lives become a true expression of our faith, and our well-being becomes an encouragement to our friends and society.

MARCH 28

Be skilful: do not make promises that you know you cannot keep. By the same token, honour the promises you have made, and never dismiss them as unimportant. Do not be depressed by misfortune and the failure to get what you want, instead be careful to see where your real profit and loss lie.

MARCH 29

Some students of religion postpone their lives and then wake up one day and say, 'Wait a minute, here I am forty years old and I don't have a spouse or a career. What am I going to do when I grow up?' They have let things back up as they wait to be enlightened or settled in mind. This shows a misunderstanding of the nature of practice.

Right Practice, the ninth step of the Eightfold Path does not involve waiting for the psyche to ripen. The clock is ticking. Right Practice is taking yourself in hand. For the lay student, it can include college, a career and a family. It is to get on with living. The confidence and maturity that comes with a productive life will enhance zazen (meditation) and deepen satori (realisation).

MARCH 30

❋

The slogan, 'Pay attention to details' is about first noticing details and then working with them. Working with the detail is a concrete way to make a big difference through a small gesture. The challenge is finding the gesture that matters, out of the many possible choices, and using that gesture to create a more healing environment. Such a healing environment doesn't spring out of thin air in full bloom; we actually have to create it – and to create it, we work with the details.

MARCH 31

❉

True cultivation depends on your true diligence. Practise at all times. There is no need to worry about where you will go after death. If you give equal weight to faith and vows in your practice, you will be fearless as to where your karma will lead you.

APRIL 1

Dear Tofu Roshi

When I meditate, I seem to exhale more completely than I inhale, and consequently, by the end of the meditation period, I feel quite deflated. What do you think I should do?

Prudence Birdwhistle

Dear Prudence

Proper breathing technique is widely misunderstood. You are not alone in having trouble with it. From your letter it sounds as though you may be making a common mistake: breathing out more times than you are breathing in.

Tofu Roshi

APRIL 2

❖

Pleasure is classified in the Buddhists texts according to its different grades and it is stated that 'the most refined and sublimest form of pleasure' is the bliss of Nirvana. This 'experience of the bliss of freedom' is so different from the conditioned pleasure and happiness of worldly existence.

APRIL 3

❋

The Buddha says: 'There are religious teachers who, because of their state of confusion, do not recognise the difference between night and day, but I would treat night as night and day as day.'

Buddhism therefore, frankly accepts the existence of both good and evil in the world of conditioned existence.

APRIL 4

A woman who respects herself and who directs her life to bringing about wholeness and freedom simply cannot establish a spiritual home in any tradition where she is not valued for who she is and what she offers. She is mature enough to distinguish the difference between authentic selflessness and self-negation. She knows that there are many things to be let go of in her quest for freedom but that inner trust and dignity are not among them.

APRIL 5

Aren't we all somewhat unrealistic and even fantasy driven? Don't we all spend too much time in foggy mental states? Don't we mess up our lives because we don't process reality as it's objectively taking place? We tell ourselves stories about our lives: we tell ourselves what we want to hear, and in doing so we create and perpetuate fantasies. This first step on the noble eightfold path tells seekers to wipe their inner wisdom eyes and discover clear vision. It tells us all that the time has come to 'get real'.

APRIL 6

❊

The less full of ourselves we are, the more room there is for others.

APRIL 7

The sexual act, if approached with the utmost sincerity, can provide a way for men and women to be transported beyond our habitual sense of finite, separate selfhood and experience a rapture that is akin to divine mystic union – even if only momentarily. Buddhist tantras present a way to take that experience and use sexual energy as a propellant to the broader and more penetrating experience of spiritual development, liberation and developing.

APRIL 8

*Let me not deceive another, or despise any being in
any state,*
*Let none through anger or ill-will wish harm upon
another.*
*Even as a mother protects with her life her child, her
only child,*
*So with a boundless heart should one cherish all
living beings,*
radiating kindness over the entire world.

In this dog-eat-dog world and impersonal market
place, consider these sterling thoughts. Hang this
quote over your desk as a reminder and enjoy a
practical application of taking refuge in the Dharma.

APRIL 9

Generosity – Giving, yielding, unconditional love – open hands, open mind, open heart.

Virtue – Ethics, honesty, morality, integrity, helping others.

Patience – Tolerance, forbearance, acceptance, forgiveness.

Effort – Energy, diligence, courage, enthusiasm, endurance.

Meditation – Concentration, focus, self-inquiry and reflection, presence of mind, mindfulness.

Wisdom – Discernment, sagacity, sanity, centredness, understanding.

APRIL 10

✵

The ignorant and the foolish think
That the fist exists separately from the pointing finger.
Mistaking the finger for the moon, they practise uselessly;
They only fabricate strange illusions in the realms of
sense and object.
Not perceiving a single Dharma; this is Tathagata (One
who has Gone Beyond misunderstanding)
Only then can one be called the supreme observer.

APRIL 11

If you do not realise Samsara and Nirvana are one,
And hold a faint idea but dimly in your mind,
In indulgence you will freely gratify your senses,
And be carried away by the torrent of desires.

APRIL 12

Mind is the coming together of three things: an outer object, an intermediary sense power and a mental consciousness.

What is the essence of that mind? The essence of mind has the qualities of emptiness, of clarity and of the two unified – where unified means that they cannot be separated. Whenever someone recognises those three qualities together that is called the experience of *rigpa*. The term *rigpa* is very sacred, very important.

APRIL 13

Your meditation must be capable of providing liberation while discursive thoughts are arising. This is so important that I will repeat this; your meditation needs to be capable of providing liberation while discursive thoughts are arising. And again, your meditation needs to be capable of providing liberation while discursive thoughts are arising!

APRIL 14

The first step in despair work is to disabuse ourselves of the notion that grief for our world is morbid. To experience anguish and anxiety in the face of the perils that threaten us is a healthy reaction. Far from being crazy, this pain is a testimony to the unity of life, the deep interconnections that relate us to all beings.

APRIL 15

The eight-spoked wheel that graces gateways and temple roofs throughout the Buddhist world symbolises the teachings of the Buddha. It is called the wheel of the Dharma, the *Dharma Chakra*. It also represents the central doctrine that his teachings convey: the doctrine of *paticca samuppada* or the dependant co-arising of all phenomena. As the Buddha said, 'They who see *paticca samuppada* see the Dharma.'

APRIL 16

Dr Ambedekar of India wrote of the Buddha:

... A reformer, full of the most earnest moral purpose and trained in all the intellectual culture of his time, who had the originality and the courage to put forth deliberately and with a knowledge of opposing views, the doctrine of a salvation to be found here, in this life, in inward change of heart to be brought about by the practice of self-culture and self-control.

APRIL 17

The Dharma wheel, as it turns now, also tells us this: that we don't have to invent or construct our connections. They already exist. We already and indissolubly belong to each other, for that is the nature of life. So, even in our haste and hurry and occasional discouragement, we belong to each other. We can rest in that knowing, and stop and breathe, and let that breath connect us with the still centre of the turning wheel.

APRIL 18

The way is an unfillable emptiness, a bottomless gulf,
that is the origin of everything in the world.

APRIL 19

The wise man wants things unwanted (by others); he does not prize things difficult to get.

APRIL 20

✳

The great way does not express itself.

APRIL 21

Zen as it is related to the mind of the haiku poet is dealt with under thirteen headings:

Selflessness.
Loneliness.
Grateful acceptance.
Wordlessness.
Non-intellectuality.
Contradictoriness.
Humour.
Freedom.
Non-morality.
Simplicity.
Materiality.
Love.
Courage.

These are some of the characteristics of the state of mind which the creation and appreciation of haiku demand.

APRIL 22

*

APRIL 23

✳

Thus from the standpoint of Zen, the Buddha 'never said a word' despite the volumes of scriptures attributed to him. For his real message remained always unspoken, and was such that, when words attempted to express it, they made it seem as if it were nothing at all. Yet it is the essential tradition of Zen that what cannot be conveyed by speech can nevertheless be passed on by 'direct pointing', by some non-verbal means of communication without which the Buddha's experience could never have been handed down to future generations.

APRIL 24

✳

The consequence of this distinction is asserted by the Zen maxim:

Great doubt: great awakening.
Little doubt: little awakening.
No doubt: no awakening.

These terse lines express how penetration of the mysterious is directly related to the degree and intensity of questioning. Doubt or questioning is seen as the indispensable key to awakening. It is the vitality of a meditative attitude, the driving force which heightens the sense of the mysterious to the point where it unexpectedly reveals what until then had remained withdrawn and unsuspected.

APRIL 25

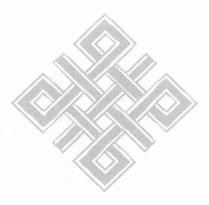

A technique of meditation is a means to achieve an end. It usually comprises a series of steps, which pass through a series of spiritual 'levels'. As a technique it belongs to the domain of calculation; its failure to produce the desired result can be treated as a problem to be solved by a reassessment of one's technical competence. A meditative attitude however is not merely a means but actually partakes in the nature of the end. It cannot be dissected into stages and levels because it is already whole and complete. It is incapable of being reduced to a technical procedure; for it belongs to the sphere of mystery and is unconcerned with the mere solving of problems.

APRIL 26

❄

Sit comfortably. Relax your body and mind and let all thoughts and worries subside. Mindfully observe your breath until you are calm and your awareness is focused in here and now.

Start by imagining all living beings around you: your mother is on your left, your father on your right, and other relatives and friends are behind you. Visualise in front of you those you dislike or who have hurt you. And extending in every direction, right to the horizon, are all other beings. Feel that they are there, all in human form, sitting quietly, like you. Stay relaxed – don't feel crowded or tense, but imagine that a sense of peace and harmony pervades everyone.

APRIL 27

Non-killing is not only important for your life, but for your family, your ethnic group, your culture and the whole of humankind. The more selfless you are, the more you care about the animal kingdom. Plants, trees and rivers are all related. That is why the first Buddhist precept dealing with not taking life is not a commandment, it is for your own good, for your own peace.

APRIL 28

How can we eliminate suffering? In Buddhism, first of all, we are encouraged to practise Dana, generosity, cutting away a bit of our selfishness. This does not just mean giving what we don't need. We should also give what is most dear to us, not only in money but also time and thought.

APRIL 29

Do not take lightly small misdeeds,
Believing they can do no harm:
Even a tiny spark of fire
can set alight a mountain of hay.

APRIL 30

Jetsun Mila sang:

> No one to ask me if I'm sick,
> No one to mourn me when I die:
> To die here alone in this hermitage
> Is everything a yogi could wish for.
>
> No trace of feet outside my door,
> No trace of blood within:
> To die here alone in this hermitage
> Is everything a yogi could wish for.
>
> No one to wonder where I've gone,
> no particular place to go.
> To die here alone in this hermitage
> Is everything a yogi could wish for.
>
> My corpse can rot and be eaten by worms,
> My gristle and bone be sucked dry by flies
> To die here alone in this hermitage
> Is everything a yogi could wish for.

MAY 1

Empty are all the Dharmas, in consequence of the
absence of own being;
  signless are all dharmas, on account of their
  signlessness;
wishless are all dharmas, because no plans are made
for the future;
  translucent in their essential original nature are all
  dharmas,
because of the perfect purity of the perfection of
wisdom.

MAY 2

❊

Because our deep desire for completion goes unsatisfied for so long, we settle for success. Or food. Or sex. Or intoxications. But none satisfies the profoundly unsatisfied for long. We settle for such small desires and just create more of the same. But our deepest desire will not be compromised, it will not settle for lesser gratification.

Only the truth that goes beyond will do. All other desires are consumed by the great desire, a yearning for the end of confusion and dulled indifference. The great desire eats all other desires.

MAY 3

❈

The suchness of pure presence does not emigrate,
migrate, transmigrate or emanate. There is no division
within pure presence. There is no multiplication of
pure presence. Suchness cannot be enumerated, even
with the numeral one.

MAY 4

One who exists solely as the boundaryless mind and heart of wisdom and love will not perceive difficulties simply because one never perceives separation, substantiality or limit.

MAY 5

❋

When the harp is played skilfully, its tones are not brought into the world from somewhere else, nor when the music finishes, do they go forth from the world to somewhere else; nor while they are resounding do they exist substantially or independently. Their exquisite beauty is the unveiling of a musical sensibility, which has been carefully trained and which depends as well on complex factors concerning the quality of the instrument and the organ of hearing.

MAY 6

All things have no real self because they come into being depending on a variety of other causes and exist in an interrelated fashion. To state a rather simple example: a bed comes from a variety of parts that are put together according to a certain design concept. There is no essence to the bed apart from its parts. When it's disassembled, that's it.

There is no longer any bed to be found; there is only the idea of 'bed' left in the mind. And even that idea or sense of 'bed' does not exist of itself but must depend on relationships with other notions or purposes, such as sleeping, reclining, a place for settling things down and empty space.

MAY 7

Question: Is the doer and the receiver (of the results) of actions one and the same?

Answer: Saying that the doer and the receiver of action are the same is an extreme view.

Question: So, the doer is one thing and the receiver another?

Answer: Saying that the doer is one thing and the receiver of actions is another is the second extreme view. The Tathagata does not attach to either of these two views and reveals the Dhamma in a middle way, saying that because ignorance is a factor, mental formations arise.

MAY 8

❖

The Buddha gives the current opinions concerning the
self as:

  (I) My self is small and has material qualities,
 (II) My self is limitless and with material qualities,
(III) My self is small and without material qualities,
(IV) My self is limitless and without material qualities.

MAY 9

❄

The basic objection to alcoholic drinks and such drugs lies in the fact that they distort the mental vision, if only temporarily; in such cases it is not possible to preserve the vigilance and alertness which Buddhists should continuously practise.

MAY 10

(The Buddha) recognises five ways of growth:

Growth in confidence based on knowledge and personal experience (*saddha*), in morality (*sila*), in learning (*suta*), in the practice of giving up things or generosity (*caga*), and in wisdom (*panna*).

MAY 11

❊

Having attained to some success, it is necessary to make it enduring. Four reasons are given for failure to do so, namely failing to seek what has been lost, not repairing what is decayed, eating and drinking to excess, and putting immoral and unreliable men or women in responsible positions.

MAY 12

I do not walk between
The step already taken
And the one I'm yet to take,
Which both are motionless.

Is walking not the motion
Between one step and the next?
What moves between them
Could I not move as I walk?

If I move when I walk,
There would be two motions:
One moving me and one my feet –
Two of us stroll by.

There is no walking without walkers,
and no walkers without walking.
Can I say that walkers walk?
Couldn't I say that they don't?

MAY 13

The Dharma taught by Buddhas
Hinges on two truths:
Partial truths of the world
And truths which are sublime.
Without knowing how they differ,
You cannot know the deep;
Without relying on conventions,
You cannot disclose the sublime;
Without intuiting the sublime,
You cannot experience freedom.

MAY 14

The fundamental Dharma of the Dharma is that there
are no Dharmas yet that this Dharma of no Dharma
is in itself a Dharma; and now that no Dharma has
been transmitted, how can the Dharma of the
Dharma be a Dharma.

Zen master Huang Po

MAY 15

Not frightened, alarmed or disturbed . . . . The Buddha states that those who are not frightened or disturbed by these teachings will be truly blessed. Across a gulf of nearly two thousand years we can see the actuate of this insight – human thinking remains addicted to categorical affirmation or denial. Our dualistic thinking continues to be the source of our greatest confusion, both personal and collective. A Buddha is a Buddha through freedom from views, from the need to affirm or deny all that is in the realm of the relative, all that is supported by linguistic conventions, but not by reality.

MAY 16

In the same soil a farmer plants two seeds: one a seed of sugar cane, the other a seed of *neem* tree, a tropical tree which is very bitter. Two seeds in the same earth, receiving the same water, the same sunshine, the same air; nature gives the same nourishment to both. Two tiny plants emerge and start growing. And what has happened to the *neem* tree? It has developed with bitterness in every fibre, while the sugar cane has developed with every fibre of it sweet. Why is nature, or if you prefer, why is God so kind to one and so cruel to the other?

MAY 17

✳

By practising Vipassana, the meditator learns not to react. At a given moment, he creates no *sankhara*; he gives no fresh stimulation to the mind. What happens then to the psychic flow? It does not stop at once. Instead one or another of the accumulated past reactions will come to the surface of the mind in order to sustain the flow. A past conditioned response will arise and from this base consciousness continues for another moment.

MAY 18

✳

The Dharma which conceals not nor reveals
Expounds the region of reality.
To realise this Dharma
Is neither ignorant nor wise.

MAY 19

Although meditation is not thinking, nevertheless it can be *clear awareness of thinking*. Thought can be a very useful object of meditation. We can turn the great power of observation on to thought itself in order to learn about its inherent nature, becoming aware of its process instead of getting lost in its content.

MAY 20

Do you see in this way how the practice we do, this simple, clear observation, is tremendously powerful? Do not undervalue the results of simply staying present with the moment's experience, and of insight into impermanence on a momentary level. The consequences for how we live and how we die are far greater than we may ordinarily realise.

MAY 21

❋

Spring comes slowly and quietly
to allow winter to withdraw
slowly and quietly.
The colour of the mountain this afternoon
is tinged with nostalgia.
The terrible war flower
has left her footprints –
countless petals of separation and death
in white and violet.
Very tenderly, the wound opens itself in the depths
of my heart. Its colour is the colour of blood,
its nature the nature of separation.

The beauty of spring blocks my way.
How could I find another path up the mountain?

. . . .

There are so many paths leading to the homeland.
They all talk to me in silence. I invoke the Absolute.
Spring has come
to every corner of the ten directions.
Its song, alas, is only the song
of departure.

This was written in 1951, less than twelve hours after
the author fell in love with a nun in Vietnam. She was
twenty. Both realised that they wanted to continue
being a monk and a nun. So they decided to depart
from each other.

MAY 22

❊

Meditation is really a non-doing. It is the only human endeavour I know of that does not involve trying to get somewhere else but, rather, emphasises being where you already are. Much of the time we are so carried away by all the doing, the striving, the planning, the reacting, the busyness, that when we stop just to feel where we are, it can seem a little peculiar at first. For one thing, we tend to have little awareness of the incessant and relentless activity of our own mind and how much we are driven by it. That is not too surprising, given that we hardly ever stop and observe the mind directly to see what it is up to. We seldom look dispassionately at the reactions and habits of our own mind, at its fears and its desires.

MAY 23

We had a question and answer period with Babaji. He never broke his vow of silence, and I am sorry to say that at times I found his answers difficult to understand, and I thought perhaps I wasn't ready for his teaching.

When I asked him how to extinguish greed, for example, he took out his teeth. What did he mean by this?

Neophyte

Dear Neophyte:

He was telling you not to bite off more than you can chew. He was also demonstrating what could happen to you if you don't floss daily.

MAY 24

Learning that love is seemingly won through our desirability, we endeavour to turn ourselves into an attractive ornament in the market place of relationship. The God of desirability is difficult to please. To earn acceptance we engage in endless occupations to mould ourselves into a model of desirability.

MAY 25

❊

Be constant amid the ebb and flow of happiness and suffering. Be friendly and even with others. Unguarded, intemperate chatter will put you in their power; excessive silence may leave them unclear as to what you mean. Keep a middle course: don't swagger with self-confidence, but don't be a doormat either. Don't run after gossip without examining the truth of it. People who know how to keep their mouth shut are rare. So don't chatter about your wishes and intentions, keep them to yourself.

MAY 26

For Vajrayana Buddhism, enlightenment is not a remote ideal but something which, with the appropriate methods and a supreme effort, can be achieved here and now, in this very life. In Tibet's living wisdom tradition, every scripture, every meditation practice and training for the mind is passed on from teacher to student, and then internalised till it becomes an integral part of that person's experience.

MAY 27

Whatever is born is impermanent and bound to die.
Whatever is stored is impermanent and is bound
to run out.
Whatever is joined is impermanent and is bound
to come apart.
Whatever is built is impermanent and is bound
to collapse.
Whatever goes up is impermanent and is bound
to fall down.

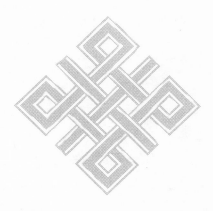

MAY 28

You remain the one final authority for your life. But as the bumper sticker says, question authority, even your own. Be flexible, be confident, and be kind to yourself as you make mistakes and follow your path. If you can learn to do this in the midst of depression, you will be able to do it at just about any time in your life, whatever situation you find yourself in.

MAY 29

❊

No matter how great a loss is, if you fully accept it straight on, the loss will turn out to be a gain. The great affair of birth and death works in a similar way. If you neither attach to nor fear birth or death, but boldly accept the reality, then you will become a liberated person in the midst of an ocean of suffering.

MAY 30

✳

Gaining enlightenment is like the moon reflecting
in the water.
The moon does not get wet, nor is the water
disturbed. Although its light is extensive
and great, the moon is reflected even in a puddle an
inch across.
The whole moon and the whole sky are reflected in
the dewdrop in the grass, in one drop of
water. Enlightenment does not disturb the
person, just as the moon does not disturb
the water.
A person does not hinder enlightenment, just as
the dewdrop does not hinder the moon.
The depth of the drop is the height of the moon.

Dogen Zenji in Genjokoan

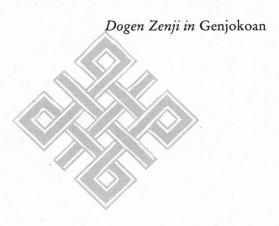

MAY 31

Daily life experiences can always be instructive. The first lesson is that destruction or obstruction are just negative terms for your context. Circumstances are like your arms and legs. They appear in your life to serve your practice. As you become more and more settled in your purpose, your circumstances begin to synchronise with your concerns. Chance words by friends, books and poems, even the wind in the trees, bring precious insights.

JUNE 1

✳

If a person believes he or she is going to die and loses hope, this emotional capitulation can itself tilt the system against recovery. Personal motivations to live are known to sometimes influence survival. Emotional disposition and support from family and friends can make a big difference in how people do in the face of serious illness.

Yet, until recently doctors did not receive much, if any, training in how to help patients make use of their own inner resources for healing, or even how to recognise when they themselves might be unwittingly undermining those very resources that are the patients' best allies in the healing process.

JUNE 2

Q: Please define 'right thinking' (more positively).

A: It means thinking solely of Bodhi (enlightenment).

Q: Is Bodhi something tangible?

A: It is not.

Q: But how can we think solely of Bodhi if it is intangible?

A: It is as though Bodhi were a mere name applied to something which, in fact, is intangible, something which never has been nor ever will be attained. Being intangible, it cannot be thought about, and it is just this not thinking about it which is called 'rightly thinking of Bodhi as something not to be thought about' – for this implies that your mind dwells upon nothing whatsoever.

JUNE 3

Q: What does right perception mean?

A: It means perceiving that there is nothing to perceive.

Q: And what does that mean?

A: It means beholding all sorts of forms, but without being stained by them, as no thoughts of love or aversion arise in the mind. Reaching this state is called 'obtaining the Buddha-eye' which really means just that and nothing else. Whereas, if the spectacle of various forms produces love or aversion in you, that is called 'perceiving them as though they had objective existence', which implies having the eye of an ordinary person, for indeed ordinary people have no other sort of eye. It is the same with all other organs of perception.

JUNE 4

❄

A Vinaya Master named Yuan once came and asked:
'Do you make efforts in your practice of the way,
Master?'

M: Yes, I do.
Q: How?
M: When hungry, I eat; when tired, I sleep.
Q: And does everybody make the same efforts as you
    do, Master?
M: Not in the same way.
Q: Why not?
M: When they are eating, they think of a hundred
    kinds of necessities and when they are going
    to sleep they ponder over affairs of a thousand
    different kinds. That is how they differ from me.

At this, the Vinaya Master was silenced.

JUNE 5

When you are alone, you might try opening your palms to the sky and holding your arms out in various positions, like branches and leaves, accessible, open, receptive, patient.

JUNE 6

❋

If you are a parent or a grandparent, try seeing the children as your teachers. Observe them in silence sometimes. Listen more carefully to them. Read their body language. Assess their self-esteem by watching how they carry themselves, what they draw, what they see, how they behave. What are their needs in this moment? At this time in their day? At this stage in their lives? Ask yourself: 'How can I help them right now?' Then follow what your heart tells you.

JUNE 7

❋

I climb the road to cold mountain,
The road to cold mountain that never ends
The valleys are long and strewn with stones;
The streams broad and banked with thick grass.
Moss is slippery, though no rain has fallen;
Pines sigh, but it isn't the wind.
Who can break from the snares of the world
And sit with me among the white clouds?

As for me, I delight in the everyday way,
Among mist-wrapped vines and rocky caves.
Here in the wilderness I am completely free,
With my friends, the white clouds, idling forever.
There are roads, but they do not reach the world;
Since I am mindless, who can rouse my thoughts?
On a bed of stone I sit, alone in the night,
While the round moon climbs up cold mountain.

Han-Shan

JUNE 8

A lightning flash –
the sound of water drops
falling through bamboo

Buson (1716–1783)
a noted painter as well as
a haiku master

JUNE 9

❋

To nourish living beings, we must not be content simply to have a virtuous diet. To save all beings, we must work tirelessly to maintain the integrity of these mandala-like places of habitat, and the people, creatures, and Buddhas who dwell in their place-like spaces.

JUNE 10

The ultimate truth, the Dhamma, is not something mysterious and remote, but the truth of our own experience. It can be reached only by understanding our experience, by penetrating it right through its foundations. This truth, in order to become liberating truth, has to be known directly. It is not enough merely to accept it on faith, to believe it on the authority of books or a teacher, or to think it out through deductions and inferences.

JUNE 11

An incredible array of devices – television, radio, newspapers, pulp journals, the cinema – turns out a continuous stream of needless information and distracting entertainment, the net effective of which is to leave the mind passive, vacant and sterile. All these developments, naively accepted as 'progress', threaten to blunt our aesthetic and spiritual sensitivities and deafen us to a higher call of the contemplative life. A serious aspirant on the path to liberation has to be very discerning in what he allows himself to be exposed to.

JUNE 12

✻

We see that the three kinds of right intentions – of renunciation, goodwill and harmlessness – counteract the three wrong intentions of desire, ill will and harmfulness. The importance of putting into practice the contemplations leading to the arising of these thoughts cannot be overemphasised. The contemplations have been taught as methods for cultivation, not mere theoretical excursions.

JUNE 13

Now when a man is truly wise,
His constant task will surely be
This recollection of his giving
Blessed with such mighty potency.

JUNE 14

If resentment arises in him when he applies his mind to a hostile person because he remembers wrong done by that person, he should get rid of the resentment by entering repeatedly into loving kindness.

JUNE 15

❋

Just as the butcher, while feeding the cow, bringing it to the shamble, keeping it tied up after bringing it there, slaughtering it and seeing it slaughtered and dead, does not lose the perception 'cow' so long as he has not carved it up and divided it into parts; but when he has divided it up and it is sitting there, he loses the perception 'cow' and the perception 'meat' occurs.

JUNE 16

One who sees only passing away and not reappearance assumes the annihilation view; and one who sees only reappearance and not passing away assumes the view that a new being appears. But since one who sees both outstrips that twofold (false) view, that vision of his is therefore a cause for purification of view.

JUNE 17

The truth of suffering should be regarded as a burden, the truth of origin as the taking up of the burden, the truth of cessation as the putting down of the burden, the truth of the path as the means to putting down the burden.

JUNE 18

To recognise that when we speak of the world we can know nothing of the person, and vice versa, actually demands only one concession: the renunciation of certainty. Language, however, is what excludes us from certainty. We have searched for certainty in the West these thousands of years, but we might as well call off the whole wasteful exercise.

JUNE 19

Do the Meditation Rock

If you want to learn how to meditate
I'll tell you now cause it's never too late
I'll tell you how cause I can't wait
it's just that great that it's never too late
If you're an old fraud like me
or a lama who lives in Eternity
The first thing you do when you meditate
is keep your spine your backbone straight
sit yourself down on a pillow on the ground
or sit in a chair if the ground isn't there.

Allen Ginsberg

JUNE 20

No wonder the Amazon burns and we do nothing, playing at business as usual while the biological fabric of life is rent asunder. No wonder our souls burn and flake with the lies, deceit, denial and brisk sale of illusion, and pardons, positive thinking and affirmations ('I deserve the luxury car of my dreams'), prosperity consciousness and expensive ecology workshops by shamans (the new age does rhyme with sewage).

JUNE 21

The kingdom of Buddha is in this world,
Within which enlightenment is to be sought.
To seek enlightenment by separating from this world
Is as absurd as to search for a rabbit's horn.
Right views are called transcendental;
Erroneous views are called worldly.
When all views, right or erroneous, are discarded
Then the essence of *Bodhi* appears
This stanza is for the Sudden school.

JUNE 22

We vow to deliver an infinite number of sentient
beings of our mind.
We vow to get rid of the innumerable defilements in
our own mind.
We vow to learn the countless systems in Dharma of
our essence of mind.
We vow to attain the supreme buddhahood of our
essence of mind.

JUNE 23

Mindfulness is often linked to a mirror; it simply reflects what is there. It is not a process of thinking; it is pre-conceptual, before thought. One can be mindful of thought. There is all the difference in the world between thinking and knowing that thought is happening, as thoughts chase each other through the mind and the process is mirrored back to us.

Mindfulness is unbiased. It is not for or against anything, just like a mirror, which does not judge what it reflects. Mindfulness has no goal other than the seeing itself. It doesn't try to add to what's happening or subtract from it, to improve it in any way.

JUNE 24

❊

We are paying full attention when there is nothing between us and the task at hand. If you are facing a sink full of dirty dishes and the mind is taken up with aversion to the task, impatience with how long it is taking, thinking about the movie you are going to see that night, you are separated from what you are doing. The hands are washing but the mind is not. To be divided this way is to be less than fully alive.

JUNE 25

✳

Now this word *Samsara* is not to be taken as referring to an endless cycle of one physical existence after another. In point of fact, it refers to a vicious circle of three events:

Desire – action in keeping with the desire – effect resulting from that action –

Inability to stop desiring – having to desire once more – action once again – another effect –

Further augmenting of desire – . . . and so on endlessly.

The Buddha called this the 'Wheel of Samsara' because it is an endless cycling on, a rolling on.

JUNE 26

It is as hard to get the children herded into the car pool and down the road to the bus as it is to chant sutras in the Buddha-hall on a cold morning. One move is not better than the other, each can be quite boring and they both have the virtuous quality of reception.

Reception and ritual and their good results come in many forms. Changing the filter, wiping noses, going to meetings, picking up around the house, washing dishes, checking the dipstick – don't let yourself think these are distracting you from your more serious pursuits.

Such a round of chores is not a set of difficulties we hope to escape from so that we may do our 'practice' which will put us on a 'path' – it is our path.

Gary Snyder
The Practice of the Wild

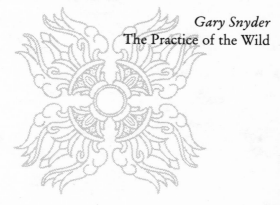

JUNE 27

Vipassana works by eradicating the grossest impurities first. When you clean a floor, first you sweep together all the rubbish and pieces of dirt, and with each succeeding sweeping you gather finer and finer dust. So in the practice of Vipassana: first the gross impurities of the mind are eradicated and subtler ones remain, which appear as pleasant sensations. However, there is a danger of developing craving for these pleasant sensations. Therefore, you must be careful not to take pleasant sensory experience as the final goal.

JUNE 28

Student: I have nothing.
Master: Then throw it away.

JUNE 29

✳

While waiting for the proper astrological moment,
benefits pass you by. Any time that benefits appear,
that is the time to seize the day – what can the stars
do?

JUNE 30

I have no parents; I make heaven and earth my
parents.
I have no divine power; I make honesty my power.
I have no means; I make submission my means.
I have no magic power; I make inward strength my
magic.
I have neither life nor death; I make eternity my life
and death.
I have no designs; I make opportunity my design.
I have no miracles; I make the way my miracle.
I have no principles; I make adaptability to all things
my principle.
I have no friends; I make my mind my friend.
I have no enemy; I make incautiousness my enemy.
I have no armour; I make goodwill my armour.
I have no castle; I make immovable mind my castle.

JULY 1

❊

The essential steps of the path to the removal of suffering – to *Nibbana* – are pointed out by the Buddha. It is the way of careful cultivation of the mind so as to produce unalloyed happiness and supreme rest from the turmoil of life. The path is indeed very difficult, but if we, with constant heedfulness, and complete awareness, walk it watching our steps, we will one day reach our destination. A child learns to stand and walk gradually and with difficulty. So too have all great ones.

JULY 2

In this modern world right livelihood can be one of the most difficult rules to obey. So many kinds of work are harmful to society and are unworthy of a true Buddhist. There are the arms and nuclear warfare industries; the drink trade; occupations involving the slaughter or vivisection of animals; yellow journalism; dishonest advertising and publicity; and business that includes usury. Buddhism is not a narrow-minded religion. It regards human frailties with understanding and sympathy. Yet the sincere Buddhist cannot profess one code of morality and earn his livelihood in an occupation with another, debased code.

JULY 3

✻

If only the love and compassion that throb through the teachings of the Buddha ruled man's action today we should not be living in the atmosphere of suspicion, fear, jealousy, arrogance, greed, hate and illusion that makes this world more and more an armed camp and drives us steadily to the brink of Armageddon.

JULY 4

An entity does not arise from itself.
It is not arisen from another.
It is not arisen from itself and another.
How can it be arisen?

JULY 5

The Buddha's teaching of the Dharma
Is based on two truths;
A truth of worldly convention
And an ultimate truth.

Those who do not understand
The distinction drawn between these two truths
Do not understand
The Buddha's profound truth

Without a foundation in the conventional truth,
The significance of the ultimate cannot be taught.
Without understanding the significance of the ultimate,
Liberation is not achieved.

JULY 6

✳

When you foist on us
All of your errors
You are like a man who has mounted his horse
And has forgotten that very horse.

JULY 7

Unexpectedly, Kendall suddenly fell into a deep coma. Everyone thought he was dying and made all the necessary arrangements. Three days later he woke up and was completely alert and responsive. After a short period of time everyone who knew him realised something had changed. The anger had disappeared and he seemed more relaxed and less self-deprecating. When the Chaplain asked him about these differences he said he was tired of hating himself. He said he had to pull all parts of himself together to face his dying.

JULY 8

Through our beliefs in an afterlife, we attempt to make death known. But the beauty (and horror) of death is that it remains unknowable. Death cannot be known because everything we know ends with death. The question is not whether there is an afterlife but what is our relationship with the unknown. There are many books which attempt to explore the after-death eperience. We can rest on these beliefs in an attempt to make death a known and safe subject, but in doing so, we misplace the real teaching of death. We may have had psychic or near-death experiences which attest to a continuation of consciousness after we die, but that is not the point. The question is, can we live without projecting anything at all on to the unknown?

JULY 9

Reflect on the nature of desire and fear. How do desire and fear project their own reality? Think about what a desire is. Does it have any reality other than a mental wish? How much of your activity is forged around wish fulfilment as opposed to accommodating things as they are.

To experience the relationship between desire and suffering, focus on any situation in which you want to have something or want something to happen. In the middle of that desire, can you settle with the situation as it is or are you forced to play out what your mind tells you or wants? See the choices before you. You can accept what reality is offering, or you can pursue your imagination.

JULY 10

Devotion is the essence of the path, and if we have in mind nothing but the guru and feel nothing but fervent devotion, whatever occurs is perceived as his blessing. If we simply practise with this constantly present devotion, this is prayer itself.

When all thoughts are imbued with devotion to the guru, there is a natural confidence that this will take care of whatever may happen. All forms are the guru, all sounds are prayer, and all gross and subtle thoughts arise as devotion.

JULY 11

✳

The purification practices, called *Ngondro* in Tibetan, have been skilfully designed to effect a comprehensive inner transformation. They involve the entire being – body, speech and mind – and begin with a series of deep contemplations on:

1. The uniqueness of human life.
2. The ever presence of impermanence and death.
3. The infallibility of the cause and effect of our actions.
4. The vicious cycle of frustration and suffering that is Samsara.

JULY 12

To awaken and develop the heart of the enlightened mind is to ripen steadily the seed of our Buddha nature, that seed that in the end, when our practice of compassion has become perfect and all embracing, will flower majestically into Buddhahood.

JULY 13

The dawning of the ground luminosity, or 'clear light', where consciousness itself dissolves into the all-encompassing space of truth. *The Tibetan Book of the Dead* says of this moment:

> The nature of everything is open, empty and naked like the sky. Luminous emptiness, without centre or circumference; the pure, naked rigpa dawns.

Padmasambhava describes the luminosity:

> The self-originated clear light, which from the very beginning was never born,
> Is the child of Rigpa, which is itself without any parents – how amazing!
> The self-originated wisdom has not been created by anyone – how amazing!
> It has never experienced birth and has nothing in it that could cause it to die – how amazing!
> Although it is evidently visible, yet there is no one there who sees it – how amazing!
> Although it has wandered through Samsara, no harm has come to it – how amazing
> Although it has seen Buddhahood itself, no good has come to it – how amazing!
> Although it exists in everyone everywhere, it has gone unrecognized – how amazing!
> And yet you go on hoping to attain some other fruit than this elsewhere – how amazing!
> Even though it is the thing that is most essentially yours, you seek for it elsewhere – how amazing!

JULY 14

To serve as a cook in the Zendo life means that the monk has attained some understanding about Zen, for it is one of the positions highly honoured in the monastery, and may be filled only by one of those who have passed a number of years here. The work is quite an irksome one, and besides, a kind of underground service which is not very much noticed by superficial observers.

JULY 15

❋

Yun-men asked a monk: What is your business now?

Monk: Nursing the sick.

Master: Do you know that there is one who never gets sick?

Monk: I do not understand.

Master: Whether you say 'yes' or whether you say 'no': it is all the same

The monk was silent.

Master: You ask me.

Monk: Who is it that never becomes sick?

The master pointed at a monk that happened to be near him.

JULY 16

The sacred truth is vast emptiness itself,
And where can one point out its marks?
Who is he who confronts me?
I know not – his answer this.

JULY 17

The Buddhist 'crazy wisdom' tradition may sound especially crazy to Westerners, and often not so wise. The crazy wisdom masters do not try to justify existence or explain it. You do not pray to anything or even do much of anything. Sometimes you hardly move. Both truth and salvation are simply a matter of being, pointing to nothing more than 'just this'.

JULY 18

We tell stories to ourselves over and over again. We bewilder and frighten ourselves, forgetting that the dismay and the fear are always about *what might have been* or what *might yet be* but what isn't happening now. We also forget that what's happening now is not going to be happening for very long.

JULY 19

It seems accurate to call meditation a 'practice', since almost nobody seems to arrive at a steady state of happiness or emptiness, or any other permanently altered condition. Nature's odds are against it. Humans are novices at mindfulness and self-realisation, and to acknowledge that truth is both forgiving and hopeful.

JULY 20

❋

You may be surprised at your inability to control the mind for even a very short time. You may be amazed to discover just how much 'chatter' goes on in there, how many images form, how much flitting from subject to subject there is, or dwelling on one issue which invades the mind over and over again. You may find that you are unable to simply sit quietly and count a few breaths. The noise and pictures just won't stop.

JULY 21

The nature of ignorance, of course, is such that we do not know that we are ignorant, otherwise we would not be so! It needs something to reveal to us, and this is where meditation comes in.

JULY 22

Q: Does our own nature include evil?

M: It does not even include good.

Q: If it contains neither good nor evil, where should we direct it when using it?

M: To set your mind on using it is a great error.

Q: Then what should we do to be right?

M: There is nothing to do, and nothing which can be called right.

JULY 23

※

If we look in the university archives, we shall see all the doctoral theses that have been written over the past one hundred years. All the hard work that has gone into writing those things, and the headaches and the anxiety and a lot of it is worthless! Now we do not get PhDs for watching the breath.

JULY 24

I used to deliberately think all the worst possible thoughts: what can I think that's the worst possible thought to think? And then I would think it. It would arise and cease in the mind. What is the best, the highest, the most altruistic, the finest thought that a human being can possibly think? And that would also arise and cease. As an experiment we can take thoughts – the worst and the best – with the deliberate intention of examining and investigating our reactions to them.

JULY 25

Loving the Buddha, saintly men go to the holy west;
Adverse to the Buddha, Bodhidharma turns his back
and comes to the east.
They met in the teahouse of illusion,
Dozing there, they lived through the dream.

JULY 26

You want to achieve something and it is achieved, but beyond that, you want acclamation, you want triumph, you want the people who opposed you to be humbled and humiliated, you want the Roman triumph where the captors were driven in front and the spoils were displayed – that is triumph! And the teacher said that this spoils the action. The action is no longer pure; it is polluted and corrupted by the desire for triumph. If this is lurking in the heart, then our actions will not be fruitful. They may seem to be effective, but in fact they are contaminated.

JULY 27

❊

Student: What is Zen?
Nan-ch'uan: Ordinary mind is very Zen.
Student: Should we try to get it?
Nan-ch'uan: As soon as you try you miss it.

JULY 28

For a man to think he was born for the sake of name and fame is a tragedy. A glance at this thing known as prestige shows it to be thoroughly insubstantial. It depends on other people having a high regard for one; and it may well be that, though no one realises it, this high regard is quite unfounded.

JULY 29

❉

The matter of 'I' and 'mine', ego and selfishness, is the single essential issue of Buddhism. The sense of 'I' and 'mine' is the one thing that must be purged completely. And it follows that in this principle lies the knowing, understanding and practice of all the Buddha's teachings, without exception.

JULY 30

Let us suppose that language is not a reflection of the world's reality. What would then happen to this whole edifice? What then would I be? What would be the self? And for sure, language does not reflect reality; it only plays games with it. This shatteringly simple repudiation of the premise of hundreds, even thousands of years of our civilisation scarcely needs any more labouring. Language, we have come to realise, has other business than reference – even reference to the 'simples' of the atomists. It is, at the lowest, a convenience of communication.

JULY 31

✳

Student: What is Zen?

Master: It is right before your eyes.

Student: So, why can't I see it?

Master: Because you have a 'me'.

Student: If I no longer have the concept 'me', will I realize Zen?

Master: If there is no 'me' who wants to realise Zen?

AUGUST 1

❊

We are not to curse and complain that the wind changed. People may be fawning on you, and then come to hate you. Someone is a bitter enemy and then, abruptly, becomes rather friendly, and you find yourselves working together. A reputation is high, and within half an hour it is lost. A man who has been ignored and despised, a woman who has been slighted, are recognised as great figures. We tend simply to hang on to this and that, but you cannot hang on, the wind changes. So, accept the changes of the wind. In the great void, there are no directions, no north or south, no east or west, no high or low.

AUGUST 2

❖

Women also need a spiritual path that speaks to our sense of ourselves biologically. Unless we choose not to have children, a great deal of time and energy is absorbed by pregnancies and childrearing. Children cannot be intellectualised: when a child needs something we must drop everything and relate to that situation concretely – if we don't, sooner or later the situation will become even more demanding and unavoidable. The life of a mother is one of constant interruptions, day and night, when the child is small. I have tried to relate to this situation in a variety of different ways in order to integrate spiritually with diapers, noise and delicate, forming hearts and minds.

AUGUST 3

❋

'Spiritual', 'mystical', 'esoteric' traditions are found in all the world's great religions: Gnosticism in Christianity; Hasidism in Judaism; Sufism in Islam; Vedanta in Hinduism; and pervasively in Buddhism. After making allowances for differences in vocabulary, symbolism and other cultural refractions, their testimonies have much in common, and constitute what has been called a 'Perennial philosophy'. Moreover, in recent years there has been a steady flow of publications from reputable physicists drawing attention to the striking parallels between the quantum revolution in subatomic physics and mystical revelation in the world's great religious traditions.

AUGUST 4

To see spiritual liberation as a personal matter that has nothing to do with politics and economics is thus as intrinsically absurd as is the opposite viewpoint. On the contrary, this is the only perspective that really can make the personal political and vice versa.

AUGUST 5

Why do we feel unhappy? It may be because we have
said or done something which has made us feel like
that. We have said something to someone, which we
now regret. We find that we feel bad about it. We may
try to justify it to ourselves, but we cannot and there
is a vague sense of shame, guilt. This feeling is the
result of what we have done. It is the karmic reaction.
If we had not intended any harm to another, we
would not be feeling like this now. Karma is quite
simple and obvious in that sense.

AUGUST 6

A characteristic of Buddhism is that it is a religion, which is not a religion. The teachings are to be used and then put down, otherwise there will be no freedom to go on. It would be regarded as foolish, for example, to hold the view that one is a 'Buddhist' and 'doing Buddhism', and of being separate and different from others who happen to follow other religions. There would be no freedom in having that kind of view. It would also be an indication that one was attached to dogma, which would be quite against the spirit of the Buddhist teachings.

AUGUST 7

A common Mantra:

OM MANI PADME HUM

'Hail to the jewel in the lotus!'
or
'Hail to the splendour (or Buddha) of your own mind!'

Those who see into their true nature
are instantaneously initiated into all the mystic teachings.

AUGUST 8

❉

One day the Buddha was giving a talk to a great assembly of monks, nuns and laypeople. At one point, he held up a flower, displayed it to the crowd and remained silent. Only Mahakasyapa, one of his monks' disciples, understood his meaning and smiled. The Buddha smiled back.

AUGUST 9

❊

'Your disciple's mind is not at peace. I beg you, master, give it rest.'

Bodhidharma said, 'Bring it to me and I will put it to rest.'

Huiko sat for a while looking for his mind, then he said, 'I have searched for the mind but have not been able to find it.'

Bodhidharma said, ' See, I have put it to rest for you then.'

AUGUST 10

In Korea, one generally practices the Koan 'What is this?'. 'What is this?' comes from an encounter between the sixth patriarch Huineng and a young monk who became one of his foremost disciples, Huaijang.

Huaijang entered the room and bowed to Huineng. Huineng asked: 'Where do you come from?'

'I come from Mount Sung,' replied Huajang.

'What is this and how did it get here?' demanded Huineng.

Huijang could not answer and remained speechless. He practised for many years until he understood. He went to see Huineng to tell him about his breakthrough.

Huineng asked: 'What is this?'

Huaijang replied: 'To say it is like something is not the point. But still it can be cultivated.'

AUGUST 11

First, we can recognise that when faced with stress, worry and conflict, we are not helpless. Buddhism has an extensive body of spiritual practices for dealing with negative emotions, based on the recognition that they always arise for a reason. Beneath their chaos and confusion, such emotions as anger and fear have an underlying logic. If we understand the cause of anger, we are well on our way to neutralising its destructive force.

AUGUST 12

※

It is often said that what distinguishes the entrepreneur is a larger tolerance for failure. Thomas Edison tried thousands of combinations of materials before he was successful in inventing the light bulb. Like most entrepreneurs, he didn't experience these disappointments as failures but as clues on the road to success.

Whether your new venture is a new job or your own business, it may fail or go through a period where it appears it may fail. Your contingency planning should include this possibility.

AUGUST 13

One mistake I made in starting my own business was underestimating the time required. The results I pictured at the end of the first year did come to pass, but not until the end of year two. I was prepared to work myself to the bone for two years, but I had to do it for three. Things take longer than we think.

Patience is an important spiritual virtue. In fact, in Buddhism it has equal standing with meditation and wisdom. But the word 'patience' implies something that is a bit too passive for what Buddhism means. In working our way through an important decision, we need acceptance, receptivity and a willingness to stay with confusion and uncertainty. It isn't just waiting, it is working.

AUGUST 14

✳

Buddhist precepts are difficult to understand. But it is not necessary to try to understand. Just receive them and form a habit of living them as a vow. It is important to have the guidance of Budddha's teaching, of the ancestors and of living teachers, all walking hand in hand with us because we don't know how to practise, how to maintain the habit of a living based on Buddha's way.

The main purpose of Buddhism is to form the habit of practice as a vow forever. This is just taking a journey in the universe, day by day, step by step. It is like walking in a mist. We don't know what the mist is, we don't know where we are walking or why; all we have to do is just walk. This is Buddha's practice.

AUGUST 15

Buddha's teaching is how we can digest our experience of the truth. To reach the peak is not the goal, because truth is emptiness. We cannot stay there, and we cannot personally hold on to the truth. The problem is if the spiritual leader holds on to the truth he has experienced and says, 'This is best', then that becomes his truth. Truth is universal, cosmic. No one can hold on to it whatever it is. If you find it let it go. This is emptiness.

AUGUST 16

✳

Almost a year ago, a dear friend of ours, Sister Ayya Khema, a German woman who is a Theravadian nun living in Sri Lanka, came to visit us and to lead a 'Vipashayana' (Insight Meditation) retreat. The retreat for me personally was something of a revelation, because she emphasised joy. I hadn't realised how much emphasis I had put on suffering in my own practice. I had focused with coming to terms with the unpleasant, unacceptable, embarrassing and painful things that I do. In the process, I had very subtly forgotten about joy.

In our seven day silent retreat, Ayya Khema taught us that each of us has in our heart a joy that's accessible to us; by connecting to it and letting it flower, we allow ourselves to celebrate our practice and our lives.

AUGUST 17

So renunciation is seeing clearly how we hold back, how we pull away, how we shut down, how we close off, and then learning how to open. It's about saying yes to whatever is put on your plate, whatever knocks on your door, whatever calls you up on your telephone. How we actually do that has to do with coming up against our edge, which is actually the moment when we learn what renunciation means.

AUGUST 18

Poetry has always been a favourite vehicle in Buddhism for speaking the wordless and revealing insight. It is also a perfect device for significant moments. The old Zen Masters would often write death poems moments before they died, or use a dramatic verse to give final instructions to their disciples.

AUGUST 19

Bowing in Zen monasteries is not only to Buddha images, it also takes place before the sitting cushion, before other people, before the meditation hall as one enters and leaves it. As Westerners, we need to understand that these are common acts of respect and gratitude in the East.

AUGUST 20

❅

Even in normal times the schedule in Zen monasteries is demanding, but on certain occasions, it is more so. This is when special intensive retreats (Sesshin) are held. Lay practitioners often join these retreats and can expect a schedule such as the following:

am
4.00 – Wake up
4.10 – Sitting meditation (Zazen)
5.00 – Walking meditation (kinhin)
5.10 – Sitting
6.00 – Chanting followed by breakfast
7.00 – Cleaning
8.10–12.00 – Alternate sessions of sitting for fifty minutes and walking for ten minutes
12.00 noon – Lunch

pm
1.00 – Working
2.10–6.00 – Alternate sessions of sitting and walking
6.00 – Supper
7.10 – Sitting
8.00 – Walking
8.10 – Sitting
9.00 – Sleep

AUGUST 21

You may not be aware that your country has been manufacturing a lot of conventional weapons to sell to third world countries for their people to kill each other. You know very well that children and adults in these countries need food more than these deadly weapons. Yet, no one has time to organise a national debate to look at the problem of manufacturing and selling these deadly things. Everyone is too busy.

AUGUST 22

Meditation is to see deeply into things, to see how we can change, how we can transform our situation. To transform our situation is to transform our minds. To transform our minds is also to transform our situation, because the situation is mind and mind is situation. Awakening is important. The nature of the bombs, the nature of injustice, the nature of the weapons, and the nature of our own beings is the same. This is the real meaning of engaged Buddhism.

AUGUST 23

During retreats, from time to time a bell Master invites the bell to sound, silently reciting the poem first:

> Body, speech, and mind in perfect oneness,
> I send my heart along with the sound of the bell.
> May the hearer awaken from forgetfulness
> And transcend all anxiety and sorrow.

Then he or she breathes three times, and invites the bell to sound. When the rest of us hear the bell, we stop our thinking and breathe in and out three times, reciting the verse:

> Listen, listen,
> This wonderful sound
> brings me back to my true self.

AUGUST 24

Once you begin to think 'has' or 'has not'
You are as good as dead.

AUGUST 25

The Buddha's way calls for energetic devotion and perseverance. When you stop to consider, however, that philosophers have been struggling for two or three thousand years to resolve the problem of human existence, without success, but that through asking 'Who am I ?' you can succeed where they have failed, have you cause to be discouraged ? What activity or work in life is more urgent or compelling than this? By comparison, everything else fades into insignificance.

AUGUST 26

✳

Famous Zen Koan:

What was your original face before your parents
were born?

AUGUST 27

A Samurai warrior approached master Hakuin and asked, 'What is hell and heaven?' The master took one look at the Samurai and started insulting him saying, 'You are such a scruffy looking warrior you would never understand anything.' The Samurai became furious and pulled out his sword. 'There!' said Hakuin. 'This is hell.'

The Samurai had a flash of illumination and was overcome with gratitude, humbly bowing before the master. Hakuin said, 'There! This is heaven.'

AUGUST 28

❊

When you think of a condemned prisoner, instead of thinking of that suffering person as someone else, imagine that it is you. Ask yourself what you would do in that situation. What now? There is nowhere to run. Nowhere to hide. No refuge and no one to protect you. You have no means of escape. You cannot fly away. You have no strength, no army to defend you. Now, at this very moment, all the perceptions of this life are about to cease. You will even have to leave behind your own dear body that you have sustained with so much care, and set out for the next life. What anguish! Train your mind by taking the suffering of that condemned prisoner upon yourself.

AUGUST 29

As much as I can, I avoid using the word 'spiritual' altogether. I find it neither useful nor necessary nor appropriate in my work at the hospital bringing mindfulness into the main stream of medicine and health care, nor in other settings in which we work such as our multi-ethnic inner city stress reduction clinic, prisons, schools and with professional organisations and athletes. Nor do I find the word 'spiritual' particularly congenial to the way I hold the sharpening and deepening of my own meditation practice.

AUGUST 30

It is important to find a teacher who has been at the practice for a while, because long experience is what brings about real learning. Finally, you need to use the kind of discernment that you use in every other aspect of your life. If a person seems authentic and dedicated, start with him or her and see how it goes.

AUGUST 31

Zen Recitation:

All things are empty.
They have no beginning and no end.
They are faultless and not faultless.
They are not perfect and not imperfect.
In this emptiness there is no form,
No perception, no names, no concepts, no knowledge.
There is no decay, nor death.
There are no four noble truths –
No suffering, no origin of suffering,
No cessation of suffering,
And no path to the cessation of suffering.
There is no knowledge of Nirvana,
No obtaining it and no not obtaining it.

SEPTEMBER 1

❉

The Four Great Vows

However innumerable beings are, I vow to save
them;

However inexhaustible the passions are, I vow
to extinguish them;

However immeasurable the dharmas are, I vow
to master them;

However incomparable the Buddha-truth is, I
vow to attain it.

SEPTEMBER 2

Do not build up your views on your senses and thoughts; but at the same time do not seek the mind away from your senses and thoughts, do not grasp the Dharma by rejecting your senses and thoughts. When you are neither attached to nor detached from, when you are neither abiding with nor clinging to, them then you enjoy your perfect unobstructed freedom, then you have your seat of enlightenment.

SEPTEMBER 3

A sculptor looks at a natural rock formation, a freshly mined slab of marble, a tree trunk, and sees the image that will reveal itself the moment strategically selected material is removed. Nothing is added to the rock, marble, or wood to create that image.

The revelation of discovery is fostered by being present, self-accepting and relaxedly alert. This can be especially important in view of the enormous pressure women, and men as well, are under as to what we should look like, feel like, feel responsible for. No wonder we often dislike ourselves for failing to measure up.

The movement of development is fostered by being present and, at the same time, making focused effort on a specific purpose.

SEPTEMBER 4

❋

Within this tree, another tree inhabits the same body; within this stone another stone rests, its many shades of grey the same, it is identical surface and weight. And within my body, another body, whose history, waiting sings: there is no other body, it sings, there is no other world.

SEPTEMBER 5

A great part of Buddhist practice is concerned with overcoming grasping at an identity, both an innate feeling of 'self' and one that is artificially created by the labels and categories that pertain to us this lifetime. I am a western nun in the Tibetan Buddhist tradition, a phrase that contains many categories. On a deeper level, however, there is nothing to grasp in being western, a nun, a Buddhist, or from the Tibetan tradition. The essence of monastic life is to let go of clinging to such labels and identities.

SEPTEMBER 6

We have to broaden our cultural perspectives from our narrow western ones and realise that this is our conditioning due to a psychology of scarcity. We have to realise that we are a success now, we've made it, we can do what we want with the world. We can wreck it if we want, but we can also run the world effectively and lovingly, and if we do run it that way, it will be cheaper and more practical. But we must stop accepting the idea that we should elect the lesser of two evils, that no government can ever do a decent job, that it's always going to be bad so why bother to vote. Democracy is the skill of people to associate with each other, to be open with each other, and not to suppress the free flow of communication, not to be authoritarian or domineering, not to be afraid of openness. It is people's ability to live in an interconnected way.

Robert Thurman

SEPTEMBER 7

It is my belief that we should courageously go beyond the narrow confines of conventional concepts and practices of social work and get to the roots of global sickness with a commitment to finding lasting remedies. After many years of working with and for people and learning from them, I have confidence in only one view. That is of people organised together as families and as small communities acting as advocates of their true interests.

Dr A.T. Ariyaratne

SEPTEMBER 8

❊

My solution for change, for those who want to make a difference, is very simple. Everyone should spend at least five to ten minutes of every day breathing deeply. I think that would make a difference, because breathing is the most important element in our lives, yet we have so little serious consideration for breathing. You don't have to believe in Buddhism; you don't have to believe in anything. If you are Christian, then breathe Christ into you. You feel peace; you breathe out with compassion, with love. I think that this is essential. For those who can take time to breathe, then I would also say to make time to meditate, in whatever spiritual tradition is right for you. In contemplation we can see the people who are suffering and can understand their suffering, can see that they are as important as we are. Then I think some seeds are planted, not only for them but also for our own benefit, as this brings very meaningful change.

Sulak Sivaraksa

SEPTEMBER 9

The significance of being human is that we have choice. We can choose to ignore anything that calls us to greater effort. Or we can begin to accept that the meaning of our life is bound up with the whole mystery of the universe. Then life itself is enhanced, for all reality comes to be seen in a new light. Each of the everyday practical things we do is enriched by a sense of ultimate meaning that brings calmness and coherence. Usually we are in a state of endless unrest, believing our lives to consist of either gaining and having or discarding and rejecting. Constantly craving and clutching, we lose sight of the state of being altogether. But when the mystical understanding of depth and otherness is there, the horizon widens and all our craving and rejections are seen in proportion, seen with steadiness and put in their own scale of time and place rather than occupying the whole of our attention.

Anne Bancroft

SEPTEMBER 10

Classification is precisely *Maya*. The word is derived from the Sanskrit root *matr-*, 'to measure, form, build or lay out a plan', the root from which we obtain such Greco-Latin words as meter, matrix, material and matter. The fundamental process of measurement is division, whether by drawing a line with the finger, by marking off or by enclosing circles with the span of the hand or dividers, or by sorting grain or liquids into measures (cups). Thus the Sanskrit root *dva* from which we get the word 'divide' is also the root of the Latin duo (two) and the English 'dual'.

SEPTEMBER 11

It is a condition of *selflessness* in which things are seen without reference to profit or loss, even of some remote, spiritual kind.

SEPTEMBER 12

❊

Without looking forward to tomorrow every moment, you must think only of this day and this hour. Because tomorrow is difficult and unfixed and difficult to know, you must think of following the Buddhist way while you live today . . . . You must concentrate on Zen Practice without wasting time, thinking that there is only this day and this hour. And that it becomes truly easy. You must forget about the good and bad of your nature, the strength or weakness of your power.

Dogen in the Shobogenzo

SEPTEMBER 13

In a universe whose fundamental principle is relativity rather than warfare there is no purpose because there is no victory to be won, no end to be attained. For every end, as the word itself shows, is an extreme, an opposite, and exists only in relation to its other ends. Because the world is not going anywhere there is no hurry.

SEPTEMBER 14

The state of Samadhi is still dualistic. When we achieve it, an inner voice says, 'This must be it!' or 'Now I'm really doing well!'

A hidden subject remains, observing a virtually blank object, in what amounts to a subject–object separation.

When we realise this separation, we try to turn on the subject as well and empty it of content. In doing so, we turn the subject into yet another object, with an even more subtle subject viewing it.

We are creating an infinite regression of subjects.

SEPTEMBER 15

❊

Whereas a concentrative practice might focus on the breath, but block out the sound of cars or the talking in our minds (leaving us at a loss when we allow any and all experience back into consciousness), awareness practice is open to any present experience – all this upsetting universe – and it helps us slowly to extricate ourselves from our emotional reactions and attachments.

SEPTEMBER 16

✢

Instead of losing myself in an upset, I notice my
thoughts and the contraction in my body. I begin to
see that the incident that upset me is not the real
problem; instead my upset arises out of my particular
way of looking at life. I pick this apart and begin to
demolish my dream. Bit by bit, I gain some perspective. My rowboat moves away from the castle I have
built, and I am no longer so caught.

SEPTEMBER 17

❋

The Great way refers to our true heart. Our true heart knows no difficulties. Our true heart refuses to make preferences. Thus, when you sit down, just sit down. It's a very simple practice. To truly sit down is to sit down in the realm of total movement, to sit along with time and place and causes and conditions.

When you just sit down, real peace immediately appears. Before any object called 'peace' appears, peace appears. So there is no room even to discuss peace. If you truly want peace, be peace right now. Peace is not simply about keeping away from weapons. Real peace is to be peace now – immediately – in this moment.

SEPTEMBER 18

We all understand that time passes from today to tomorrow. But we don't understand at all that time also passes from today to yesterday. Actually, time passes away from this moment in all directions. As Dogen mentions, time also passes from today to today, because today is morning, afternoon, evening and night. They seem separate, but in their simultaneity they're not.

SEPTEMBER 19

✳

If we are going to take care of our suffering, we have to know the true face of reality. For this, we must deepen our lives. We need wisdom. This wisdom is a function of the human heart and mind. It is our innate capacity to see beyond the dualistic world of greed and anger, to where we may learn to live in peace and harmony with all beings. This is not to escape the dualistic world. It is to take care of the dualistic world.

SEPTEMBER 20

There are two ways to take care of your life. You can develop yourself as an artist, or you can forget yourself and devote your life to art. That's a big difference. The first is to enslave yourself in your ego. It feels good for a while, but it doesn't last for long. This is to become a host for the guest. The second way is to become a host for the host. You must turn your ego into fuel and burn your life for the benefit of all beings. You will become a kind of fool. But this is the way to find peace. Just climb the mountain every day.

SEPTEMBER 21

❋

In Buddhism a spiritual life requires the practice of taking a vow. Mahayana Buddhists take the vow of the Bodhisattva, which has four parts: to taste truth, to save all beings, to master the teachings of the Buddha, to accomplish the Buddha way.

SEPTEMBER 22

Institutional religion is the form which a traditional teaching assumes in order to be able to act from the objective material order of things subjectively upon the hearts and minds of men. All the outward, organisational and social supports of the doctrine, such as temples, monastic orders, vestments, canonical languages, sacred art and music, together with traditional customs and observance of every kind, are to be included under this aspect. So far as Buddhism is concerned, personal religion covers the study, understanding and practice of the teachings pertaining to morality, meditation and wisdom.

SEPTEMBER 23

In the wake of mindfulness and self-possession comes contentment. The monk is described as being content with the robe that protects his body and the bowl in which he collects food. 'Wherever he goes,' says the beautiful simile of the Pali texts, 'he is provided with these two things; just as a winged bird in flying carries his wings along with him.' At least in principle, contentment is a virtue that can be practised regardless of the number of one's possessions, by a householder no less than by a monk, by a prince as easily as by a pauper.

SEPTEMBER 24

※

The great bliss queen has two hands, signifying the two prerequisites for enlightenment: method, especially compassion and concentration, and wisdom. Her red colour signifies her passionate dedication to training disciples. Her nakedness indicates that she has overcome the obstructions to liberation from cyclic existence and the obstructions to full understanding of everything knowable, and that she is free from the clothing of conceptualisation that conceives subject and dualistically. Her manner of standing, with two feet placed evenly on the ground, signifies that she dwells neither exclusively in mundane existence nor in the peaceful disappearance into the nature of reality. One foot is placed slightly in front of the other, an indication of her readiness to act for others.

SEPTEMBER 25

Never until today has such a wealth and variety of Buddhist resources – texts, practices and living teachers – been made available in so short a period of time to populations who are at the same time so ignorant of the cultures from which these traditions have come.

SEPTEMBER 26

Our children are with us so briefly. They change so quickly. What we do now helps to mould them and their future families, and *their* future families. To be mindful in what we do requires intention and effort. To give our own true mind to the intricacies of family relationships is a Buddha field to practice in. If we can be happy and peaceful within our families, it can't help but impact our wider world. If we neglect the opportunities to practise with our families, that too can't help but impact our wider world.

SEPTEMBER 27

Although one cannot bring children up as Buddhists (since to follow the Buddha's path has to be the free choice of the individual) one can surround them with positive influences – and what can be better for a child than to have around her- or himself adults who are fulfilled, growing as individuals, and trying to lead an ethical life?

SEPTEMBER 28

Message recited to Dharma students:

Life and death are of supreme importance
Time passes swiftly and
Opportunity is lost.
Each of us must strive
To awaken,
Take heed.
Do not squander your lives.

SEPTEMBER 29

Zen Master:

If you meet the Buddha, kill him.

SEPTEMBER 30

✳

Basho's Enlightenment:

> A still pond,
> A frog jumps in
> Kerplunk.

OCTOBER 1

It is undeniably easier to ignore the hardships of those who are too weak to demand their rights than respond sensitively to their needs. To care is to accept responsibility, to dare to act in accordance with the dictum that the ruler is the strength of the helpless.

OCTOBER 2

❊

Authoritarian governments see criticism of their actions and doctrines as a challenge to combat. Opposition is equated with 'confrontation', which is interpreted as violent conflict.

Regimented minds cannot grasp the concept of confrontation as an open exchange of major differences with a view to settlement through genuine dialogue. The insecurity of power based on coercion translates into a need to crush all dissent.

OCTOBER 3

✤

With right contemplation, the illusion of body and
mind vanishes.
With purity, and perfect clarity, the Buddha realm is
illuminated.

OCTOBER 4

When one is awakened, it is just because of the original existence of awakening. It is not that you formerly lost it and now you have first attained it, or that you had rejected it before and now you have selected it. When you are deluded, it is just because delusion is already present. It is not that you had formerly attained it and now you have for the first time lost it. Nor is it that before you had selected it and now you have rejected it. Attaining and losing, selecting and rejecting are nothing but the deluded projections of sentient beings. The nature of enlightenment is originally present: its existence or non-existence does not depend upon delusion and awakening.

OCTOBER 5

It is explained that all the things which are mentioned as being liable to birth are also liable to ageing: disease, dying, sorrow and stain. We are attached to family, possessions, gold and silver, to everything we believe can give us pleasure. We long for what is pleasant and we have aversion when we do not get what we want. Our attachment is a source of endless frustrations.

OCTOBER 6

The kind of civilisation which is exerting its influence over the entire world today is founded on the basic premise that mankind is separate from nature. According to this view mankind is nature's owner, free to manipulate nature according to his will. In the present time we are beginning to see that many of the problems arising from material progress, particularly the environmental ones, are rooted in this basic misconcept.

OCTOBER 7

❉

Without skilful reflection, human beings are utterly swamped by the influence of external factors, such as religious beliefs, traditions and social values. It is easy to see how traditions and customs mould human attitudes. Most people are completely swayed by these things, and this is the karma that they accumulate.

OCTOBER 8

Searching for data and personal histories to support the issue of life after death has some benefits, and such doings should not be discouraged, but to say that ethical practice must depend on their verification is neither true nor desirable.

OCTOBER 9

❊

I teach householders to look at the cause of *dukkha* (suffering) in daily life and to see that often it is not external. It does not have to do with anyone in particular when you feel angry, upset or disappointed. It is usually yourself that feeds these emotions. The root cause is within.

OCTOBER 10

When true confidence arises in the Dhamma, it gives great impetus to the practice. Such a jewel is worth more than any precious thing in the whole world because it enables us to surpass and transcend all worldly problems and difficulties. They do not disappear, but we no longer recognise them as a hindrance because we have seen absolute truth.

OCTOBER 11

❉

This is one of the very important aspects of the ability to enter into the meditative absorptions: namely that no matter what happens in one's daily life, independent of outside triggers, the external conditions, the mind knows it can attain this pleasure, of which the Buddha said, 'This is a pleasure I will allow myself.'

OCTOBER 12

✳

We Buddhists must find the courage to leave our temples and enter the temples of human experience, temples that are filled with suffering. If we listen to the Buddha, Christ and Gandhi, we can do nothing else. The refugee camps, the ghettos and the battle-fields will then become our temples. We have so much work to do.

Prah Maha Ghosananda
from Peace is Every Step

OCTOBER 13

On the one hand the sacred is infinite, timeless and transcendent; on the other hand it is the pattern to be followed. By being both transcendent and yet realisable it compels the religious person to gain distance from personal situations, to be unattached to the pressures of the particular moment and to feel at one with universal and higher values. The symbol reveals the transcendent to the religious person.

OCTOBER 14

❊

The image of the jewel net of Indra, for instance, is an illustration of the essential Buddhist understanding that existence is a mutual interfusion and interpenetration of all phenomena. The doctrine of 'mutual penetration' is symbolised by a vast net. In every interstice is a brilliant jewel in which is reflected all the other individual jewels as well as the entire net. But these are not identical jewels, an infinite expanse of beautiful gems of mind-numbing uniformity. Rather each jewel is a symbol for a unique phenomenon, utterly individual and distinct from all others, yet at the same time 'containing' them all.

OCTOBER 15

❋

The spiritual essence comes into consciousness by way of symbol. Thus symbols function at the threshold of the passage from time to eternity. Religious symbols can be images, metaphors, deities which when uncorrupted are transparent to the worldless realm, the realm of transcendence. They can be seen in self-luminous dreams, and when this happens they appear not to be part of the mind's organised conceptual system.

OCTOBER 16

You are the golden eternity because there is
no me and no you, only one golden eternity.

This world is the movie of what everything is,
it is one movie, made of the same stuff
throughout, belonging to nobody, which is what
everything is.

Sociability is a big smile, and a big smile is
nothing but teeth. Rest and be kind.

Jack Kerouac
from The Scripture of the Golden Eternity

OCTOBER 17

✳

BODHISATTVA VOWS

BODDHISATTVA VOWS TO BE THE LAST ONE
OFF THE SINKING SHIP – YOU SIGN UP AND
FIND OUT IT'S FOREVER – PASSENGER LIST
ENDLESS – SHIP NEVER EMPTIES – SHIP KEEPS
SINKING BUT NEVER GOES QUITE UNDER – ON
BOARD ANGST, PANIC AND DESPERATION
HOLD SWAY – TURNS OUT BODHISATTVAHOOD
IS A FUCKING JOB LIKE ANY OTHER BUT
DIFFERENT IN THAT THERE'S NO WEEKENDS,
HOLIDAYS, VACATIONS, NO GOLDEN YEARS OF
RETIREMENT – YOU'RE SPENDING ALL YOUR
TIME AND ENERGY GETTING OTHER PEOPLE
OFF THE SINKING SHIP INTO LIFEBOATS
BOUND GAILY FOR NIRVANA WHILE THERE
YOU ARE SINKING – AND OF COURSE YOU HAD
TO GO AND GIVE YOUR LIFEJACKET AWAY – SO
NOW LET US BE CHEERFUL AS WE SINK – OUR
SPIRIT EVER BUOYANT AS WE SINK.

Albert Saijo

OCTOBER 18

❄

Gathas

When the children fight in the car
I vow with all beings
to show how the car doesn't move
unless all of its parts are engaged.

When I'm drawn to watch crime on TV
I vow with all beings
to smile at my own little drama
and expose the killer of time.

If action must wait for a satori
I vow with all beings
to forget satori completely.
What a relief! Let's go home!

When someone speaks of no self
I vow with all beings
to be sure there is no contradiction –
the speaker is there after all.

Hearing the crickets at night
I vow with all beings
to find my place in the harmony
crickets enjoy with the stars.

Robert Aitken

OCTOBER 19

❉

Painting to be constructed in your head

Go on transforming a square canvas
in your head until it becomes a
circle. Pick out any shape in the
process and pin up or place on the
canvas an object, a smell, a sound,
or a colour that comes to your mind
in association with the shape.

Yoko Ono

OCTOBER 20

❋

To Bodhi Dharma

O Great Mountain Bodhidharma
First Cloud-driver in China
Opening the way of vast emptiness
Nothing holy.
We are still inspired every day
By your gutsy honesty.
You dared to be yourself
And just don't know.

Tenshib Reb Anderson

OCTOBER 21

In a famous simile the Buddha Master was fond of, the practitioner is like a patient, the Dharma is like the medicine, the mentor is the physician who analyses the patient's sickness, and prescribes a specific medicine, and the practice of the Dharma is the therapy.

OCTOBER 22

Since all the violence there is,
The terror and suffering in the world,
All come from this habit of the self,
What can I do with this great devil?

If I don't give myself up completely,
I won't be able to abandon suffering,
just as you can't stop burning yourself
As long as you don't let go of the fire.

Shantideva

OCTOBER 23

❋

Through my ambition to achieve
The supreme of goals,
Far better than any wish-granting gem,
May I always deeply cherish every being!

Geshe Langri Tangpa Dorjey Sengey

OCTOBER 24

The Tibetans use an image I have found helpful. They liken the mind to a great clear sky, a cloudless sky. All the phenomena of mind and body are happenings in this clear sky. They are not the sky itself. The sky is clear and unaffected by what is happening. The clouds come and go, the winds come and go, the rain and sunlight all come and go, but the sky remains clear. Make the mind like a big clear sky and let everything arise and vanish on its own. Then the mind stays balanced, relaxed, observing the flow.

OCTOBER 25

Another great help in rousing mindfulness is slowing down. Slow down your actions. Make every moment of the body all day long an object of meditation. From the moment of getting up to the moment of going to sleep, notice everything very clearly, very sharply: every moment in bathing, in dressing, in eating. Our habitual way of doing things is to rush, toppling forward into the next moment or next activity, being always in transition. Make an effort to settle back into the moment. There's no hurry. There is no place to go.

OCTOBER 26

The human heart has the extraordinary capacity to hold and transform the sorrows of life into a great stream of compassion. It is the gift of figures like Buddha, Jesus, Mother Mary and Kwan Yin, the Goddess of Mercy, to proclaim the power of this tender and merciful heart in the face of all the suffering of the world. Whenever your own heart is open and uncovered, the awakening of this stream of compassion begins within. Compassion arises when you allow your heart to be touched by the pain and need of another.

OCTOBER 27

It is a basic principle of spiritual life that we learn the deepest things in unknown territory. Often it is when we feel most confused inwardly and are in the midst of our greatest difficulties that something new will open. We awaken most easily to the mystery of life through our weakest side. The areas of our greatest strength, where we are the most competent and clearest, tend to keep us away from the mystery. To go into this territory beyond our own self, to enter these realms without a guide, can be like trying to lift ourselves by our own bootstraps.

OCTOBER 28

As for celibacy within marriage, remember that like sex, celibacy is more meaningful when you do it with someone else. If you begin to feel rejected, remind yourself that your wife wants to be celibate with you.

OCTOBER 29

After settling yourself in your posture and turning your attention to your breath, again sense in your body the entire movement of your breath from beginning to end. Notice the slight pause between the ending of one out breath and the beginning of the next in breath. Let your attention move in harmony with the movement of each breath, following its progress from your nostrils to your abdomen and the movements of your body as the breath is released. Notice the sensation of your breath as it enters your body and passes through your throat, the expansion and contraction of your chest, and rise and fall of your abdomen. When distracted, again simply return your attention to the next breath to begin again.

OCTOBER 30

❊

In order to experience the ultimate truth of liberation, it is necessary first to penetrate beyond apparent reality and to experience the dissolution of body and mind.

OCTOBER 31

❄

Faith in the Mind

The Way is perfect like vast space
Where nothing is lacking and nothing is in excess.
Indeed, it is due to our choosing to accept or reject
that we do not see the true nature of things
nor in inner feelings of emptiness.
Be serene in the oneness of things
and such erroneous views will
disappear by themselves.
When you try to stop activity to achieve passivity
your very effort fills you with activity
as long as you remain in one extreme or the other
you will never know . . .

Seng-ts'an

NOVEMBER 1

A life of wisdom can be looked at from two perspectives: inwardly, it is characterised by serenity, cheerfulness, awareness and freedom. Experiencing an agreeable sensation, the mind is not intoxicated or deluded by it. When deprived of comforts, the mind is firm, unshaken and untroubled. Happiness and suffering are no longer invested into external objects.

NOVEMBER 2

For the unenlightened being, experiences and situations are normally interpreted and evaluated through the following biases or influences:

1. The concern for desires for the five kinds of sense objects (sights, sounds, smells, tastes and bodily sensations)
2. The concern for the existence and preservation of the self, its identities and desired situations (bhava)
3. Views, beliefs and ways of thinking (ditthi)
4. Delusion or ignorance (avijja): not clearly knowing the meaning of things as they are, which leads to the perception of self.

NOVEMBER 3

It should be stressed that the inter-determination within a chain of events does not necessarily have to be in sequential order, just as chalk, a blackboard and writing are all indispensable determinants for the white letters on a blackboard's surface, but do not have to appear in sequential order.

NOVEMBER 4

Now we as volunteer workers should be motivated by the highest altruistic motives. Our minds should always vibrate with love for the entire living world, which we call Sarvodaya, the awakening of all.

A. T. Ariyaratne

NOVEMBER 5

✣

Exploitation, whether indulged in by individuals, groups, societies, organisations or governments, has to be realised by the people in practical terms before an attempt is made to end such exploitative processes.

A.T. Ariyaratne

NOVEMBER 6

❊

These three factors (Right speech, Right Action and Right Livelihood) of the Eightfold Path constitute ethical conduct. It should be realised that the Buddhist ethical and moral conduct aims at promoting a happy and harmonious life both for the individual and for society. This moral conduct is considered as the indispensable foundation for all higher spiritual attainments. No spiritual development is possible without this moral basis.

NOVEMBER 7

It is the vague feeling 'I AM' that creates the idea of self which has no corresponding reality, and to see this truth is to realise Nirvana, which is not very easy.

NOVEMBER 8

❉

The common belief that to follow the Buddha's teaching one has to retire from life is a misconception. It is really an unconscious defence against practising it. There are numerous references in Buddhist literature to men and women living ordinary, normal family lives who successfully practised what the Buddha taught, and realised Nirvana.

NOVEMBER 9

If one thing does not exist without another, and does exist when that also exists, then that other thing is really its cause. How can that be called an obstacle?

Santideva

NOVEMBER 10

✳

When those who do not understand the Dharma act improperly, they look left and right to make sure no one is looking. How foolish! The Buddha, the Dharma, our karma, are always watching. Do you think the Buddha cannot see that far? We never really get away with anything.

NOVEMBER 11

Practice begins here and now. Suffering and liberation, the entire path, are here and now. The teaching, words like virtue and wisdom, only point to the mind. But these two elements, path and defilement, compete in the mind all the way to the end of the path. Therefore, applying the tools of practice is burdensome, difficult – you must rely on endurance, patience and proper effort. Then true understanding will come about on its own.

NOVEMBER 12

When you are conscious of fear, it no longer frightens you. Only by heedlessly resisting it does fear gain strength in your life. When you recognise the fact that fear is only a condition, it becomes like a dragon. It looks capable of harming you, but when you actually confront it, the dragon suddenly shrivels up and is no longer threatening.

NOVEMBER 13

We have intelligent, critical minds, so we think about ourselves in very negative ways. We criticise ourselves because a lot of the things we have done in the past come up in the present – memories, tendencies or habits – and they don't live up to what we would like them to be. Likewise we don't live up to what we think we should be.

NOVEMBER 14

With insight meditation we are not picking and choosing. We are allowing everything – even trivialities – to arise in consciousness, and we are letting them go. We are recognising conditions purely as conditions. So it is a compassionate thing we are doing. We are not grasping at each thing as if it were a real being or person or as 'ours'.

NOVEMBER 15

The self may not be something, but neither is it nothing. It is simply ungraspable, unfindable. I am why I am not because of an essential self hidden away in the core of my being, but because of the unprecedented and unrepeatable matrix of conditions that have formed me.

NOVEMBER 16

*

Traditionally patience is classified into three types: the patience of forgiveness, the patience of accepting suffering, and the patience of being able to behave virtuously.

NOVEMBER 17

All water in the ocean has a taste of salt. So too, whatever extensive discourses the Buddha delivered, all were aimed at liberation and deliverance from defilements.

NOVEMBER 18

Everyone should uphold the teachings of practice leading to realisation because realisation and liberation are the essence of Buddhism. This is what the Buddha really taught. Every person is capable of that realisation because truth is inherent in every being. The one who practises sincerely is the one who upholds Buddhism. This is the highest merit.

NOVEMBER 19

For those who are prepared, strict intensive meditation is extremely useful. If it is combined with isolation, the meditator can quickly develop strong concentration and clear insight.

NOVEMBER 20

Meditation has one object only, namely to prepare the mind to get out of all suffering, to prepare it for liberation. It is a means to this end and not for pleasant experiences.

NOVEMBER 21

Happiness which arises through concentration is based upon purity. A similar happiness can be experienced in one's daily life if purity has been cultivated. In the meditative practice pleasant feelings, happiness and equanimity become deeper and more profound than in daily living, but unless one has already attained some purity in one's ordinary life, one won't be able to do it in meditation either. Daily living and meditation go hand in hand.

NOVEMBER 22

The Buddha said that some people are born in the light and go to the light. Some people are born in the light and go to the dark. Some people are born in the dark and go to the light. Some people are born in the dark and go to the dark. This means that no matter where we are born, our choices and opportunities exist.

NOVEMBER 23

I try to greet all these visitors and new arrivals from Tibet in person. Invariably, our meetings are very emotional; most are such sad innocent people, ragged and destitute. I always ask them about their own lives and families. And always there are tears when they reply – some breaking down as they relate their pitiful stories.

NOVEMBER 24

In general, we Tibetans are very religious minded and there are many who are good practitioners as well, but believing the country would be saved without human effort, through prayers alone, resulted from limited knowledge.

The Dalai Lama

NOVEMBER 25

✳

Overall I have found much that is impressive about Western society. In particular, I admire its energy and creativity and hunger for knowledge. On the other hand, a number of things about the Western way of life cause me concern. People there have an inclination to think in terms of 'black and white' and 'either, or' which ignores the facts of interdependence and relativity. Between two points of view they tend to lose sight of the grey areas. Also, with thousands of brothers and sisters for neighbours, so many people appear to be able to show their true feelings only to their cats and dogs.

The Dalai Lama

NOVEMBER 26

✲

Despotic governments do not recognise the precious human component of the state, seeing its citizens only as a faceless, mindless – and helpless – mass to be manipulated at will. It is as though people were incidental to a nation rather than its very lifeblood. Patriotism, which should be the vital love and care of a people for their land, is debased into a smokescreen of hysteria to hide the injustices of authoritarian rulers who define the interests of the state in terms of their own limited interests.

NOVEMBER 27

❄

'Where are you from?' asked the frog that lived in the well.

'I come from the great ocean,' the visitor replied.

'How big is this ocean of yours?' asked the frog from the well.

'It is enormous,' replied the other.

'About a quarter the size of my well?' he asked.

'Oh! Bigger than that!' exclaimed the frog from the ocean.

'Half the size then?'

'No, bigger than that!'

'So – the same size as the well?'

'No, no! Much, much bigger!'

'That's impossible,' said the frog who lived in the well. 'This I have to see for myself.'

NOVEMBER 28

Think about a piece of music – some great symphony – we don't expect it to get better as it develops, or that its whole purpose is to reach the final crescendo. The joy is found in listening to the music in each moment.

NOVEMBER 29

As a young monk, Dogen (1200–1253) was obsessed with the question:

'Why do we have to practise Buddhism if we already have Buddha nature?'

NOVEMBER 30

When you are enlightened, you realise that there is no inside or outside of the mind.

DECEMBER 1

❉

A verse of Shen-hsiu, who had not seen his true nature

> The body is like a bodhi tree,
> and the mind a mirror bright
> carefully we wipe them every day
> and let no dust alight.

A verse of Hui-Neng, who had seen his true nature

> The body is not like a bodhi tree
> and there there is no mirror bright
> since everything is empty to begin with
> where can the dust alight?

DECEMBER 2

Working with obstacles is life's journey. The warrior is always coming up against dragons. Of course the warrior gets scared, particularly before the battle. It's frightening. But with a shaky, tender heart, the warrior realises that he or she is just about to step into the unknown, and then goes forth to meet the dragon. The warrior realises that the dragon is nothing but unfinished business presenting itself, and that it's fear that really needs to be worked with.

DECEMBER 3

In the Uttara Tantra by Maitreya, our Buddha nature is described as being like a golden statue wrapped in filthy rags. Our innate potential is to awaken this nature like discovering a precious jewel buried in the depth of the earth. Buddha nature is predominantly pure, but obscured by our karmic debris accumulated over countless lifetimes.

DECEMBER 4

The thought manifests as the word.
The word manifests as the deed.
The deed develops into the habit.
The habit hardens into the character.
The character gives birth to the destiny.
So, watch your thoughts with care
And let them spring from love
Born out of respect for all beings.

DECEMBER 5

All Dharmas arise from causes and conditions. When the cause and conditions exist, the result occurs accordingly.

Who has created this? It is the law of nature. When it breaks up, it is also nature. This law is called Dharma.

DECEMBER 6

If you have looked at Buddhist art, you've noticed that many representations of the Buddha or other embodiments have decidedly feminine characteristics: breasts, delicate facial features, softly draped clothing. Buddhists believe that, as beings achieve more refined levels of enlightenment, the distinctions of sex and gender fall away leaving a transgender or genderless figure.

DECEMBER 7

There are four topics to consider when contemplating how to rely on a spiritual guide:

1. The advantages of properly relying on a spiritual guide
2. The disadvantages of not relying on one or relying on one incorrectly
3. How to rely on one by means of our thoughts
4. How to rely on one by means of our actions.

DECEMBER 8

*

When suffering strikes, our first desire is for the situation to be different. When we suffer a loss the first thing we are inclined to do is to deny that it has happened. 'This cannot be real,' we tell ourselves. Then the next thing that happens is we feel angry. We try to escape by blaming others, but the blaming generally makes the situation worse.

DECEMBER 9

❅

Who am I? What am I?
Listen! There may be no answer in words,
The answer may be in the silence;
The answer may be in the questions;
Who am I? What am I?

DECEMBER 10

Tantra challenges the reasonably low opinion of human potential by showing us how to view ourselves and all others as transcendentally beautiful, as gods and goddesses in fact. One of the essential practices at all levels of Tantra is to dissolve our ordinary concepts of ourselves and then, from the empty space into which these concepts have disappeared, arise in the glorious light body of a deity.

DECEMBER 11

I have the impressions that Buddhists prefer committing themselves to ethically unproblematic issues like rainforests, whales, primal people, animal rights, even human rights and world peace – and to all forms of service – rather that involving themselves with the militant wretched of the earth (especially close to home) and with the structural violence of our social system.

Ken Jones

DECEMBER 12

A person who is suffering may sometimes be helped more by a gentle walk through beautiful countryside, by seeing smiling faces and beautiful flowers, than by recounting a catalogue of misfortunes which have beset them in life. We do need to do something about the weeds which grow in our garden, but it is necessary to water the good seeds too.

DECEMBER 13

✳

We could say that compassion is the ultimate attitude of wealth: an anti-poverty attitude, a war on want. It contains all sorts of heroic, juicy, positive, visionary, expansive qualities. And it implies larger scale thinking, a freer and more expansive way of relating to yourself and the world.

DECEMBER 14

We often find ourselves in situations completely
naked, wishing we had clothes to cover ourselves.
These embarrassing situations always come to us in
life.

Q: Must we have a spiritual friend before we can
   expose ourselves or can we just open ourselves to
   the situations of life?
A: I think you need someone to watch you do it,
   because then it will seem more real to you. It is
   easy to undress in a room with no one else around
   but we find it difficult to undress ourselves in a
   room full of people.

DECEMBER 15

One must also examine fear and expectation. If there is fear of death one examines that; if one fears old age, one examines that. If one feels uneasy about a certain ugliness in oneself, or a certain disability or physical weakness of any kind, one examines them as well. And one should also examine one's mental image of one's self, and anything one may feel bad about. It's very painful in the beginning.

DECEMBER 16

Let us accept that the Buddha knew the truth when he said everyone has seven underlying tendencies: sensual desire, ill-will, speculative views, sceptical doubt, conceit, craving for continued existence and ignorance. We can find them in ourselves, smile at them and say, 'Well there you are. I'll do something about you.'

DECEMBER 17

Instead of being hopeful you develop another attitude, which is that of the warrior. If a warrior lives within hope, that makes him a very weak warrior. He is still concerned with his success. If the warrior has no longer the hope of achieving success, he has nothing to lose. Therefore enemies find it very difficult to attack him. The warrior will also regard the defeat as a victory, since he has nothing to lose.

DECEMBER 18

'What must I do, then?' I asked thoughtfully.

'You must learn to wait properly.'

'And how does one learn that?'

'By letting go of yourself, leaving yourself and everything of yours behind you so decisively that nothing more is left of you but a purposeless tension.'

DECEMBER 19

All the delightful things of the world – sweet sounds, lovely forms, all the pleasant tastes and touches and thoughts – these are all agreed to bring happiness, if they are not grasped and possessed.

But if you regard them merely as pleasures for your own use and satisfaction and do not see them as passing wonders, they will bring suffering.

DECEMBER 20

Someone asked Buddha,
Are you a god?
No, I am not a god.
Are you a deva?
No I am not a deva.
Are you a human being?
No I am not a human being.
Then what are you?
I am awakened.

DECEMBER 21

The most basic fear experienced by people coming to see me for therapy is of being overwhelmed by the force of their own emotion if they relax the grip of their egos. They fear that if they give up control, they will lose control, that their unconscious will, if given a chance, rise up and inundate them. In some way, this reflects the classic view of the unconscious as a seething cauldron of demonic forces that have to be tamed by the light of reason and analysis.

DECEMBER 22

The Whole world is tormented by words
And there is no one who does without words.
But in so far as one is free from words
Does one really understand words?

Saraha
from Treasury of Songs

DECEMBER 23

We can also cause a great deal of pain to other people if we selfishly gratify our sexual cravings without taking others' needs into account. Buddhists therefore try to see sexual partners as important individuals with their own wants, needs and fears, and never descend to exploiting others as sex objects in however subtle a way. This might include, for example, not entering into unequal relationships where the partner is likely to have expectations we have no intention of fulfilling.

DECEMBER 24

Buddhism contemplates the reform of the whole world. It acts upon the contemplation. To do so it trains people. This training aims for genuine spiritual autonomy. It has a sudden aspect and a gradual progressive aspect. The gradual aspect is character building. This sudden aspect may be called a change of heart. It does not necessarily involve spiritual pyrotechnics. If there is a change of behaviour supported by a change of heart, then there is something reliable.

DECEMBER 25

The hard truth is that spiritual realisation is relatively easy compared with the much greater difficulty of actualising it, integrating it fully into the fabric of one's embodiment and one's daily life. By *realisation*, I mean the direct recognition of one's ultimate nature, while *actualisation* refers to how we live in all the situations of our life.

DECEMBER 26

✻

The nature of phenomena is non dual,

but each one, in its own state, is beyond
the limits of the mind.

There is no concept that can define
the condition of 'what is'

But vision nevertheless manifests:
all is good.

Everything has already been accomplished,
and so, having overcome the sickness of effort,

one finds oneself in the self-perfected state:
this is contemplation.

DECEMBER 27

So the purpose of practice is to seek inwardly, investigating until you reach the original mind. Original mind is also known as pure mind. It is the mind without attachment. It isn't affected by mental objects and doesn't chase after pleasant and unpleasant phenomena. Rather, it is in a state of continuous wakefulness, thoroughly aware of all its experiences.

DECEMBER 28

Spiritual work brings to light and helps us release this attachment to limited notions of who we are, so that we may realise our larger nature, which lies beyond all form, structure or thought. If psychotherapy is like pruning and fertilising a tree so it can grow up and bear fruit, spiritual practice is more radical medicine. It goes to the roots – the root clinging to a limited concept of self.

DECEMBER 29

Heart Sutra

Form is Emptiness and the very Emptiness is Form;
Emptiness is no other than form, form is no other
than emptiness.
Whatever is form, that is emptiness; whatever is
emptiness, that is form.
The same is true of feelings, perceptions, impulses
and consciousness.
All dharmas are empty of own being, are without
marks; they are neither
produced nor stopped, neither defiled nor
immaculate, neither deficient nor complete . . .

DECEMBER 30

❖

GONE, GONE, GONE BEYOND,
GONE ALTOGETHER BEYOND
O WHAT AN AWAKENING
ALL HAIL.

Avolokita

DECEMBER 31

It is said that when the Buddha attained his enlightenment under the bo tree, he exclaimed in amazement that all beings are inherently enlightened, we just don't know it. He taught that it is only our own confusion which veils us from our natural wisdom and goodness.

Glossary

Attachment: clinging to pleasure, views, rituals and oneself. Freedom means the end of such attachments, not the end of kindness, compassion and connection.

Becoming: constantly going on to something different or wanting to become something different. 'Becoming' refers to what has become now or what will or might become in the future and the self's relationship to becoming.

Bodhi: enlightenment, awakening, supreme knowledge of the complete resolution of suffering.

Bodhicitta: consciousness that is directed towards enlightenment.

Bodhisattva: a Buddha-to-be, one who lives with deep compassion and aspires to complete enlightenment.

Buddha: literally, an Awakened One.

Consciousness: the inner factor of the mind that enables us to be a conscious human being.

Conditioned: causes and factors that affect any aspect of existence and produce change whether we like it or not.

Delusion: includes confusion, fantasies, fears, getting caught up in self-image, etc.

Dependent arising: e.g. a motorcar depends upon numerous parts that are dependently arising together for it to be called a car. 'Dependently arising' applies to everything and everyone.

Desire: wanting for experiences, things, etc., which grips the mind.

Deva: a radiant being who is happy and lives in a heavenly way but is not enlightened.

Dharma: teachings of the Buddha, the truth, duty, the nature of things.

Discipline: to follow and apply the Dharma to one's daily life.

Emptiness: absence of any real inherent substance to phenomena due to dependent arising. Synonym for 'Freedom'. Emptiness implies the Inexpressible and Inconceivable. Emptiness makes everything possible.

Enlightenment: realisation of an indestructible liberation, the emptiness of the ego, a profound opening of the heart, and wisdom about existence.

Equanimity: the capacity to stay steady in the face of unhealthy patterns and towards pleasurable objects of desire; the capacity to stay steady in the face of painful situations or non-significant situations.

Evil: the deliberate volition to cause great suffering and pain to others.

Faculties: physical and mental features and qualities.

Form: what has shape, such as body and material things.

Formations: various states of mind and thoughts that arise due to various patterns and tendencies.

Formless: space, consciousness, etc.

Gods: evolved spiritual beings.

Gone beyond: not trapped in the world of birth and death and events between the two polarities.

Haiku: a succinct Zen poem of a set number of syllables, which reveals a great truth.

Heaven: a long but temporary period of joy and happiness.

'I' and *'mine':* egotism, cherish of self, self-importance, self-condemnation.

I am: in terms of Dharma, indicates a grasping on to a sense of self as if 'I am unique and separate from all else'.

Ignorance: literal translation is 'not knowing'. Means not seeing clearly, so problems and suffering arise in our life.

Immaterial and limited: e.g. consciousness.

Immaterial and unlimited: e.g. experience of consciousness of oneself as the consciousness of all.

Impurity (in reference to the body): literal translation is 'absence of what is beautiful'.

Karma: unsatisfactory influences from the past that make an impact on the present and generate further volitions and actions in body, speech and mind.

Knowing: indicates a profound knowing in daily life of a true and unshakeable freedom.

Mara: the force of temptation that leads to difficulties.

Material form: includes the physical body and all objects in our surroundings.

Material and limited: e.g. a state of being such as the body.

Material and unlimited: e.g. experience of oneness with everything else.

Meditative concentration: meditation to ground oneself in the here and now, to see clearly into the nature of things, development of calm and insight into 'I', 'me' and 'mine'.

Nirvana: liberation from living in greed, hate and delusion. 'Nirvana' is immediately realisable here and now in the midst of life. The ultimate peace that also expresses a fulfilled and awakened life.

Noble Student or Noble One: a transformed person, who knows freedom and lives wisely.

One Thus Gone: reference to an enlightened one. Such a one has gone beyond clinging, wanting, standpoints, egotism and sense of limitation imposed by mind and body.

Patticca samuppada: dependent arising; a wide variety of conditions enabling phenomena to arise.

Practice: three-fold inner development through ethics, meditation and wisdom.

Rebirth: the Buddha generally has accepted the doctrine of unresolved forces like waves arising in the ocean of existence. On a couple of occasions, he has adopted a provisional view of belief in rebirth.

Rigpa: 'brightness'; a Tibetan term to signify a profound experience of clear consciousness free from obscuring states of mind.

Sangha: men and women who have realised a noble transformation.

Sankhara: formations; usually referring to formations of mind through wholesome and unwholesome activity

Sutra: discourse or talk.

Unbecoming, Unborn, Unconditioned, Unmade: synonyms for Liberation or True Freedom that is not made nor dependent on circumstances for its presence. Fulfilment of the spiritual life.

Unconditioned: frequent simile for Liberation or Nirvana. Steady, sublime and unaffected in the midst of things.

Unwholesome: what causes problems for oneself and others through patterns of mind and behaviour.

Vipassana: 'insight'; a meditation discipline to see directly into the body/mind process to realise liberation through insight.

Wholesome: what brings about benefits for oneself and others.

Useful Addresses

For further information about Buddhist retreat centres, write to the following organisations.

Beatenburg Meditation Zentrum
Beatenburg Waldegg
Postfach 54
CH 3803
Switzerland

Insight Meditation Society
1230 Pleasant Street
Barre,
MA 01005
USA

Gaia House
West Ogwell
Newton Abbot
Devon TQ12 6EN
England
e-mail:
generalenquiries@gaiahouse.co.uk
www.gaiahouse.co.uk
www.insightmeditation.org

Spirit Rock Meditation Centre
PO Box 909
Woodacre
CA 94973
USA.

Index

Entries are given with full publication details on their first occurrence; where the same book has been used again, only the author and page number is given, and the reader is referred back to the day on which the book is first mentioned for full publication details. Names in italic in the main text refer to those quoted in the works listed below.

January 23: Patrul Rinpoche, *The Words of My Perfect Teacher*, HarperCollins Publishers, San Francisco, CA, USA, 1994, p.252

January 24: Patrul Rinpoche, as for Jan 23, p.275

January 25: Ajahn Sumedho, *The Mind and the Way*, Rider Books, London, UK, 1995, p.55

January 26: Ajahn Sumedho, as for Jan 25, p.125

January 27: Philip Martin, *The Zen Path through Depression*, HarperCollins Publishers, New York, USA, 1999, pp.58,59

January 28: Thich Nhat Hanh, *Call Me by My True Names*, Parallax Press, CA, USA, 1993, p.127

January 29: Ch'an Master Sheng-Yen, *Complete Enlightenment*, Dharma Drum Publishers, USA, 1997, p.143

January 30: Buddhadasa Bhikkhu, as for Jan 20, p.27

January 31: Garma C.C. Chang (trans.), as for Jan 10. p.106

February 1: Patrul Rinpoche, as for Jan. 23, p.105

February 2: Patrul Rinpoche, as for Jan. 23, p.130

February 3: Timothy Freke, as for Jan. 18, p.89

February 4: Timothy Freke, as for Jan. 18, p.102

February 5: Buddhadasa Bhikkhu, *No Religion*, Sublime Life Mission, Bangkok, Thailand, 1979, p.20

February 6: Buddhadasa Bhikkhu, as for Feb. 5, p.31

February 7: Stephen Batchelor, *Alone with Others: An Essential Approach to Buddhism*, Grove Weidenfield, New York, USA, p.41

February 8: Stephen Batchelor, as for Feb. 7, p.81

February 9: Sharon Salzberg, *Loving Kindness: The Revolutionary Art of Happiness*, Shambhala Publications, Boston, USA, 1995, p.35

February 10: Sharon Salzberg, as for Feb 9, p.41

February 11: Sharon Salzberg, as for Feb 9, p.94

February 12: Sharon Salzberg, as for Feb 9, p.156

February 13: Padmasiri De Silva, *The Ethics of Moral Indignation and the Logic of Violence: A Buddhist Perspective*, the Public Trustee Department, Sri Lanka, 1934, p.21

February 14: Akong Tulki Rinpoche, *Taming the Tiger*, Rider Books, London, UK, 1994, p.64

February 15: K. Venkata Ramanan, as for Jan. 22, p.106

February 16: Susan Suntree, *Wisdom of the East: Stories of Compassion, Inspiration and Love*, Contemporary Books, USA, 2002, p.40

February 17: John Seed, *Thinking Like a Mountain*, Heretic Books, USA, 1988, p.105

February 18: Larry Rosenberg, *Breath by Breath: The Liberating Practice of Insight Meditation*, Shambhala Publications, Boston, USA, 1998, p.82

February 19: Larry Rosenberg, as for Feb. 18, p.54

February 20: Thanissaro Bhikkhu, *The Wings to Awakening*, Dhamma Dana Publication, Barre, MA, USA, 1996, p.36

February 21: Thanissaro Bhikkhu, as for Feb 20, p.81

February 22: Bernie Glassman, *Infinite Circle*, Shambhala Publications, Boston, MA, USA, 2002, p.46

February 23: Bernie Glassman, as for Feb 22, p.83

February 24: Bhante Walpola Piyananda, *Saffron Days in LA: Tales of a Buddhist Monk*, Shambhala Publications, Boston, MA, USA, 2001, p.81

February 25: Timothy Freke, as for Jan 18, p.109

February 26: Carole Tonkinson (ed.), *Big Sky Mind: Buddhism and the Beat Generation*, HarperCollins Publishers, London, UK, 1995, p.43

February 27: Carole Tonkinson (ed.), as for Feb. 26, p.310

February 28: Carole Tonkinson (ed.), as for Feb. 26, p.101

March 1: Ajahn Chah, *Bodhinyana: Teachings of Ajahn Chah*, Sangha Publications, Thailand, 1980, p.44

March 2: Ajahn Chah, as for Mar. 1, p.146

March 3: Nyoshul Khenpo, *Natural Great Perfection*, Snow Lion Publications, USA,1995, p.98

March 4: Nyoshul Khenpo, as for Mar. 3, p.151

March 5: Nyoshul Khenpo, as for Mar. 3, p.23

March 6: P.A. Payutto, *Good, Evil and Beyond: Kamma in the Buddhist Teaching*, Buddhadhamma Foundation, Thailand, 1993, p.69

March 7: Mark Epstein MD, *Thoughts without a Thinker*, Basic Books, New York, USA, 1995, p.20

March 8: Mark Epstein MD, as for Mar. 7, p.93

March 9: Mark Epstein MD, as for Mar. 7, p.102

March 10: Venerable Ajahn Sumedho, *The Four Noble Truths*, Amaravarti Publications, Bangkok, Thailand, 1992, p.47

March 11: Venerable Ajahn Sumedho, as for Mar. 10, p.66

March 12: Nyanaponika Thera, *The Heart of Buddhist Meditation*, Rider, London, UK, 1969, p.40

March 13: A.F. Price and Wong Mou-Lam (eds.), *The Diamond Sutra and the Sutra of Hui Neng*, Shambhala Publications, CA, USA, 1969, p.13

March 14: A.F. Price and Wong Mou-Lam, as for Mar 13, p.91

March 15: Buddhadhasa Bhikkhu, *Handbook for Mankind: Principles of Buddhism*, Sublime Life Mission, Bangkok, Thailand, p.3

March 16: Shunryu Suzuki, *Zen Mind, Beginners Mind: Informal talks on Zen Meditation and Practice*, Weatherhill Inc., New York, USA, 1996, p.31

March 17: Shunryu Suzuki, as for Mar. 16, p.21

March 18: Shunryu Suzuki, as for Mar. 16, p.47

March 19: Shunryu Suzuki, as for Mar. 16, p.84

March 20: Sharon Salzberg, *Voices of Insight*, Shambhala Publications, Boston, MA, USA, 1999, p.214

March 21: Sharon Salzberg, as for Mar. 20, p.252

March 22: Susan Murcott, *The First Buddhist Women: Translations and Commentary on the Therigatha*, Parallax Press, CA, USA, 1991, p.87

March 23: Susan Murcott, as for Mar. 22, p.106

March 24: Susan Murcott, as for Mar. 22, p.126

March 25: Thich Nhat Hanh, *Living Buddha, Living Christ,* Riverhead Books, New York, USA, 1995, p.95

March 26: Thich Nhat Hanh, as for Mar. 25, p.108

March 27: Thich Nhat Hanh, as for Mar. 25, p.113

March 28: Dudjom Rinpoche, *Counsels from my Heart*, Shambhala Publications, Boston, MA, USA, 2001, p.79

March 29: Robert Aitken, *Encouraging Words*, Pantheon Books, USA, 1993, p.85

March 30: Judith L. Lief, *Making Friends with Death*, Shambhala Publications, Boston, MA, USA, 2001, p.138

March 31: Ch'an Master Sheng-Yen, *Dharma Drum: The Life and Heart of Ch'an Practice*, Dharma Drum Publications, USA, 1996, p.162

April 1: Susan Moon, *The Life and Letters of Tofu Roshi*, Shambhala Publications, Boston, MA, USA, 1998, p.13

April 2: K.N. Jayatilleke, *Ethics in Buddhist Perspective*, Buddhist Publication Society, London, UK, 1972, p.19

April 3: K.N. Jayatilleke, as for Apr. 2, p.30

April 4: Christina Feldman, *Woman Awake: A Celebration of Women's Wisdom*, Penguin Group, London, UK, 1989, p.57

April 5: Lama Surya Das, *Awakening the Buddha Within*, Broadway Books, New York, USA, 1997, p.98

April 6: Lama Surya Das, as for Apr. 5, p.180

April 7: Lama Surya Das, as for Apr. 5, p.212

April 8: Lama Surya Das, as for Apr. 5, p.239

April 9: Lama Surya Das, as for Apr. 5, p.273

April 10: Chan Master Sheng-Yen, *The Poetry of Enlightenment*, Dharma Drum Publications, New York, USA, 1992, p.62

April 11: Garma C.C Chang, as for Jan. 10, p.197

April 12: Tony Duff, *Ground, Path and Fruition: Collected Teachings of the Venerable Tsoknyi Rinpoche*, Padma Karpo Translation Committee, Nepal, 1997, p.65

April 13: Tony Duff, as for Apr. 12, p.64

April 14: Joanna Macy, *World as Lover, World as Self*, Parallax Press, CA, USA, 1991, p.21

April 15: Joanna Macy, as for Apr. 14, p.53

April 16: Joanna Macy, as for Apr. 14, p.163

April 17: Joanna Macy, as for Apr. 14, p.242

April 18: R.H. Blyth, *Haiku: Volume 1, Eastern Culture*, Hokuseido Press, Tokyo, 1984, p.40

April 19: R.H. Blyth, as for Apr. 18, p.41

April 20: R.H. Blyth, as for Apr. 18, p.43

April 21: R.H. Blyth, as for Apr. 18, p.154

April 22:

April 23: Alan W. Watts, *The Way of Zen*, Thames and Hudson, UK, 1957, p.45

April 24: Stephen Batchelor, *The Faith to Doubt: Glimpses of Buddhist Uncertainty*, Parallax Press, CA, USA, 1990, p.44

April 25: Stephen Batchelor, as for Apr. 24, p.57

April 26: Kathleen McDonald, as for Jan. 3, p.95

April 27: Sulak Sivaraksa, *When Loyalty Demands Dissent*, Santi Pracha Dhamma Institute, Bangkok, Thailand, 1993, p.222

April 28: Sulak Sivaraksa, as for Apr. 27, p.240

April 29: Patrul Rinpoche, as for Jan 23, p.239

April 30: Patrul Rinpoche, as for Jan 23, pp.243,244

May 1: Edward Conze (trans.), *Perfect Wisdom: The Short Prajnaparamita Texts*, Buddhist Publication Group, Totnes, Devon, England, 1993, p.188

May 2: Stephen Levine, *Guided Meditations, Explorations and Healings*, Doubleday, New York, USA, 1991, p.127

May 3: Lex Hixon, *Mother of the Buddhas: Meditation of the Prajnaparamita Sutra*, The Theosophical Publishing House, USA, 1993, p.35

May 4: Lex Hixon, as for May 3, p.47

May 5: Lex Hixon, as for May 3, p.222

May 6: Phra Prayudh Payutto/Grant A. Olson, *Buddhadhamma: Natural Laws and Values for Life*, State University of New York Press, USA, 1995, p.90

May 7: Phra Prayudh Payutto/Grant A. Olson, as for May 6, p.141

May 8: Ven. Hammalawa Saddhatissa, *Buddhist Ethics*, Wisdom Publications, London, UK, 1987, p.31

May 9: Ven. Hammalawa Saddhatissa, as for May 8, p.95

May 10: Ven. Hammalawa Saddhatissa, as for May 8, p.127

May 11: Ven. Hammalawa Saddhatissa, as for May 8, p.130

May 12: Stephen Batchelor, *Verses from the Center: A Buddhist Vision of the Sublime*, Riverhead Books, UK, 2000, p.84

May 13: Stephen Batchelor, as for May 12, p.123

May 14: Mu Soeng, *The Diamond Sutra: Transforming the Way We Perceive the World*, Wisdom Publications, Boston, MA, USA, 2000, p.94

May 15: Mu Soeng, as for May 14, p.119

May 16: William Hart (ed.), *The Art of Living: Vipassana Meditation as Taught by S.N. Goenka*, Harper and Row Publishers, San Francisco, CA, USA, 1987, p.42

May 17: William Hart (ed.), as for May 16, p.109

May 18: Lu K'uan Yu (Charles Luk), *Ch'an and Zen Teaching: Second*

Series, Rider and Company, London, UK, 1961, p.40

May 19: Joseph Goldstein, *Insight Meditation: The Practice of Freedom*, Gill and Macmillan Ltd, Boston, MA, USA 1993, p.59

May 20: Joseph Goldstein, as for May 19, p.167

May 21: Thich Nhat Hanh, as for Jan. 28, p.94

May 22: Jon Kabat-Zinn, *Full Catastrophe Living: Using the Wisdom of Your Body and Mind to Face Stress, Pain and Illness*, Delacorte Press, Bantman Doubleday Dell Publishing Group Inc. New York, USA, 1990, p.60

May 23: Susan Moon, as for Apr. 1, p.54

May 24: Christina Feldman, as for Apr. 4, p.61

May 25: Dudjom Rinpoche, as for Mar. 28, p.79

May 26: Patrul Rinpoche, as for Jan 23, p.xxxii

May 27: Patrul Rinpoche, as for Jan 23, p.46

May 28: Philip Martin, as for Jan 27, p.88

May 29: Ch'an Master Sheng-Yen, as for Mar. 31, p.161

May 30: Bernie Glassman, as for Feb. 22, p.94

May 31: Robert Aitken, *The Practice of Perfection*, Pantheon Books, USA, 1994, p.70

June 1: Jon Kabat-Zinn, as for May 22, p.187

June 2: John Blofeld, *Zen Teaching of Instantaneous Awakening: Master Hui Hai*, Buddhist Publishing Group, Devon, England,1995, p.40

June 3: John Blofeld, as for Jun. 2, p.41

June 4: John Blofeld, as for Jun. 2, p.83

June 5: Jon Kabat-Zinn, *Wherever You Go There You Are: Mindfulness Meditation in Everyday Life*, Hyperion, USA, 1994, p.150

June 6: Jon Kabat-Zinn, as for Jun. 5, p.256

June 7: Stephanie Kaza and Kenneth Kraft, *Dharma Rain: Sources of Buddhist Environmentalism*, Shambhala Publications, Boston, MA, USA, 2000, p.54

June 8: Stephanie Kaza and Kenneth Kraft, as for Jun 7, p.56

June 9: Stephanie Kaza and Kenneth Kraft, as for Jun 7, p.306

June 10: Bhikkhu Bodhi, *The Noble Eightfold Path, Buddhist Publication Society*, Sri Lanka, 1984, p.83

June 11: Bhikkhu Bodhi, as for Jun. 10, p.57

June 12: Bhikkhu Bodhi, as for Jun. 10, p.43

June 13: Bhadantacariya Buddhaghosa, *The Path of Purification*, A. Semage, Colombo, Ceylon, 1964, p.243

June 14: Bhadantacariya Buddhaghosa, as for Jun. 13, p.324

June 15: Bhadantacariya Buddhaghosa, as for Jun. 13, p.381

June 16: Bhadantacariya Buddhaghosa, as for Jun. 13, p.465

June 17: Bhadantacariya Buddhaghosa, as for Jun. 13, p.586

June 18: Maurice Ash, *Journey into the Eye of a Needle*, Green Books, Devon, England, 1989, p.36

June 19: Allan Hunt Badiner, *Dharma Gaia: A Harvest of Essays in*

Buddhism and Ecology, Parallax Press, CA, USA, 1990, p.213

June 20: Allan Hunt Badiner, as for Jun. 19, p.225

June 21: A.F. Price and Wong Mou-Lam (eds), as for Mar. 13, p.87

June 22: A.F. Price and Wong Mou-Lam (eds), as for Mar. 13, p.102

June 23: Larry Rosenberg, as for Feb. 18, p.15

June 24: Larry Rosenberg, as for Feb. 18, p.169

June 25: Buddhadasa Bhikkhu, as for Mar. 15, p.32

June 26: Jon Kabat-Zinn, as for Jun. 5, p.172

June 27: William Hart, as for May 16, p.113

June 28: Timothy Freke, as for Jan. 18, p.52

June 29: Phra Prayudh Payutto/Grant A. Olson, as for May 6, p.154

June 30: Timothy Freke, as for Jan. 18, p.63

July 1: Piyadassi Thera, *The Buddha's Ancient Path*, Rider and Company, London, UK, 1964, p.76

July 2: Piyadassi Thera, as for Jul. 1, p.157

July 3: Piyadassi Thera, as for Jul. 1, p.125

July 4: Jay L. Garfield, *Nagarjuna's Mulamadhyamakakarika: The Fundamental Wisdom of the Middle Way*, Oxford University Press, New York, USA, 1995, p.53

July 5: Jay L. Garfield, as for Jul. 4, p.68

July 6: Jay L. Garfield, as for Jul. 4, p.69

July 7: Rodney Smith, *Lessons from the Dying*, Wisdom Publication, USA, 1998, p.53

July 8: Rodney Smith, as for Jul. 7, p.84

July 9: Rodney Smith, as for Jul. 7, p.135

July 10: Sogyal Rinpoche, *The Tibetan Book of Living and Dying*, HarperCollins Books, New York, 1992, p.149

July 11: Sogyal Rinpoche, as for Jul. 10, p.155

July 12: Sogyal Rinpoche, as for Jul. 10, p.201

July 13: Sogyal Rinpoche, as for Jul. 10, p.259

July 14: Daisetz Teitaro Suzuki, *The Training of the Zen Buddhist Monk*, Wingbow Press, CA, USA, 1974, p.47

July 15: Daisetz Teitaro Suzuki, as for Jul. 14, p.51

July 16: Daisetz Teitaro Suzuki, as for Jul. 14, p.97

July 17: Wes Nisker, *The Essential Crazy Wisdom*, Ten Speed Press, CA, USA, 2001, p.44

July 18: Sylvia Boorstein, *It's Easier Than You Think*, HarperCollins Publishers, San Francisco, CA, USA, 1997, p.68

July 19: Wes Nisker, *Buddha's Nature*, Rider Book, London, UK, 1998, p.21

July 20: Diana St Ruth, *Experience Beyond Thinking: A Practical Guide to Buddhist Meditation*, Buddhist Publishing Group, Totnes, UK, 1996, p.54

July 21: Diana St Ruth, as for Jul 20, p.27

July 22: John Blofeld, as for Jun 2, p.105

July 23: Ajahn Sumedho, *Teachings of a Buddhist Monk*, Buddhist Publishing Group, Totnes, UK, 2000, p.59

July 24: Ajahn Sumedho, as for Jul. 23, p.95

July 25: Trevor Leggett, *The Old Zen Master: Inspiration for Awakening*, Buddhist Publishing Group, Totnes, UK, 2000, p.62

July 26: Trevor Leggett, as for Jul. 25, p.63

July 27: Timothy Freke, as for Jan. 18, p.14

July 28: Buddhadasa Bhikkhu, *Why Were We Born?* Sublime Life Mission, Bangkok, Thailand, 1974, p.7

July 29: Buddhadasa Bhikkhu, as for Jan. 1, p.5

July 30: Maurice Ash, as for Jun. 18, p.43

July 31: Timothy Freke, as for Jan. 18, p.87

August 1: Trevor Leggett, as for Jul. 25, p.112

August 2: Tsultrim Allione, *Women of Wisdom*, Routledge and Kegan Paul Plc, London, UK 1984, p.18

August 3: Ken Jones, *Beyond Optimism: A Buddhist Political Ecology*, Jon Carpenter Publishing, Oxford, UK, 1993, p.40

August 4: Ken Jones, as for Aug. 3, p.44

August 5: Diana and Richard St Ruth, *Simple Guide to Theravada Buddhism*, Global Books Ltd, Kent, UK, 1998, p.55

August 6: Diana and Richard St Ruth, as for Aug. 5, p.38

August 7: Diana St Ruth, *An Introduction to Buddhism,* Buddhist Publishing Group, Devon UK, 1998, p.56

August 8: Martine Batchelor, *Thorsons Way of Zen*, Thorsons, London UK, 2001, p.23

August 9: Martine Batchelor, as for Aug. 8, p.26

August 10: Martine Batchelor, as for Aug. 8, p.94

August 11: Lewis Richmond, *Work as a Spiritual Practice: A Practical Buddhist Approach to Inner Growth and Satisfaction on the Job*, Broadway Books, New York, USA, 1999, p.31

August 12: Lewis Richmond, as for Aug. 11, p.176

August 13: Lewis Richmond, as for Aug. 11, p.177

August 14: Dainin Katagiri, *Returning to Silence: Zen Practice in Daily Life*, Shambhala Publications Ltd, Boston, MA, USA, 1988, p.94

August 15: Dainin Katagir, as for Aug. 14, p.112

August 16: Pema Chodron, *The Wisdom of No Escape and the Path of Loving Kindness*, Shambhala Publications, Boston, MA, USA, 1991, p.24

August 17: Pema Chodron, as for Aug. 16, p.53

August 18: Diana and Richard St Ruth, *The Simple Guide to Zen Buddhism*, Global Books Ltd, Kent, UK, 1998, p.59

August 19: Diana and Richard St Ruth, as for Aug. 18, p.70

August 20: Diana and Richard St Ruth, as for Aug. 18, p.74

August 21: Thich Nhat Hanh, *Being Peace*, Parallax Press, CA, USA, 1987, p.72

August 22: Thich Nhat Hanh, as for Aug. 21, p.74

August 23: Thich Nhat Hanh, as for Aug. 21, p.105

August 24: Roshi Philip Kapleau, *The Three Pillars of Zen* (25th Anniversary Edn), Anchor Books, Doubleday, New York, USA, 1989, p.77

August 25: Roshi Philip Kapleau, as for Aug. 24, p.147

August 26: Timothy Freke, as for Jan 18, p. 27

August 27: Timothy Freke, as for Jan 18, p.39

August 28: Patrul Rinpoche, as for Jan 23, pp. 201, 202

August 29: Jon Kabat-Zinn, as for Jun. 5, p.263

August 30: Larry Rosenberg, as for Feb. 18, p.172

August 31: Timothy Freke, as for Jan 18, p.107

September 1: D.T. Suzuki, *Manual of Zen Buddhism*, Rider and Company, London, UK, 1950, p.14

September 2: D.T. Suzuki, as for Sep. 1, p.118

September 3: Marianne Dresser, *Buddhist Women on the Edge: Contemporary Perspectives from the Western Frontier*, North Atlantic Books, CA, USA, 1996, p.41

September 4: Marianne Dresser, as for Sep. 3, p.321

September 5: Marianne Dresser, as for Sep. 3, p.228

September 6: Eddie and Debbie Shapiro, *Voices from the Heart*, Tarcher/ Putman Books, New York, USA, 1992, p.39

September 7: Eddie and Debbie Shapiro, as for Sep. 6, p.91

September 8: Eddie and Debbie Shapiro, as for Sep. 6, p.140

September 9: Eddie and Debbie Shapiro, as for Sep. 6, p.350

September 10: Alan W. Watts, *The Way of Zen*, Thames and Hudson, UK, 1957, p.39

September 11: R.H. Blyth, as for Apr. 18, p.155

September 12: Alan W. Watts, as for Sep. 10, p.158

September 13: Alan W. Watts, as for Sep. 10, p.175

September 14: Charlotte Joko Beck, *Nothing Special: Living Zen*, Harper San Francisco, CA, USA, 1993, p.85

September 15: Charlotte Joko Beck, as for Sep. 14, p.171

September 16: Charlotte Joko Beck, as for Sep. 14, p.141

September 17: Dainin Katagiri, *You Have to Say Something: Manifesting Zen Insight*, Shambhala Publications, Boston, MA, USA, 1998, p.78

September 18: Dainin Katagiri, as for Sep. 17, p.48

September 19: Dainin Katagiri, as for Sep. 17, p.75

September 20: Dainin Katagiri, as for Sep. 17, p.115

September 21: Dainin Katagiri, as for Sep. 17, p.147

September 22: Sangharakshita, *A Survey of Buddhism*, Shambhala Publications Inc, MA, USA, 1980, p.179

September 23: Sangharakshita as for Sep. 22, p.139

September 24: Ann Carolyn Klein, *Meeting the Great Bliss Queen: Buddhists, Feminists, and the Art of*

Self, Beacon Press, Boston, MA, USA, 1996, p.181

September 25: Ann Carolyn Klein, as for Sep 25, p.195

September 26: Sandy Eastoak, *Dharma Family Treasures: Sharing Mindfulness with Children, An Anthology of Buddhist Writings*, North Atlantic Books, CA, USA, 1994, p.71

September 27: Sandy Eastoak, as for Sep. 26, p.91

September 28: Judith Blackstone and Zoran Josipovic, as for Jan 11, p.88

September 29: Judith Blackstone and Zoran Josipovic, as for Jan 11, p.92

September 30: Judith Blackstone and Zoran Josipovic, as for Jan 11, p.133

October 1: Aung San Suu Kyi, *Freedom from Fear*, Penguin Books, New Delhi, India, 1991, p.172

October 2: Aung San Suu Kyi, as for Oct. 1, p.176

October 3: A. Charles Muller, *Commentary by the Son Monk Kihawa: The Sutra of Perfect Enlightenment, Korean Buddhism Guide to Meditation*, State University of New York Press, USA, 1999, p.101

October 4: A. Charles Muller, as for Oct. 3, p.117

October 5: Nina Van Gorkom, *Cetasikas*, Zolag, 1999, p.213

October 6: P.A. Payutto, as for Mar. 6, p.63

October 7: P.A. Payutto, as for Mar. 6, p.67

October 8: P.A. Payutto, as for Mar. 6, p.51

October 9: Martine Batchelor, *Walking on Lotus Flowers: Buddhist Women Living, Loving and Meditating*, Thorsons/HarperCollins Publisher, London, UK, 1996, p.58

October 10: Ayya Khema, *When the Iron Eagle Flies: Buddhism for the West*, Penguin Group, London, UK, 1991, p.75

October 11: Ayya Khema, *Being Nobody, Going Nowhere: Meditations on the Buddhist Path*, Wisdom Publications, Boston, MA, USA, 1987, p.119

October 12: Ven. Maha Ghosananda, *Step by Step*, Parallax Press, Berkeley, C, USA, 1992, p.63

October 13: Anne Bancroft, *A Map of Hidden Treasures: Spiritual and Religious Symbolism*, The Sharpham Papers, Devon, UK, 1993, p.6

October 14: Anne Bancroft, as for Oct. 13, p.12

October 15: Anne Bancroft, as for Oct. 13, p.9

October 16: Gary Gach, *What Book!? Buddha Poems from Beat to HipHop*, Parallax Press, CA, USA, 1998, p.14

October 17: Gary Gach, as for Oct. 16, p.19

October 18: Gary Gach, as for Oct. 16, p.93

October 19: Gary Gach, as for Oct. 16, p.105

October 20: Gary Gach, as for Oct. 16, p.164

October 21: Robert Thurman, *Essential Tibetan Buddhism*, HarperCollins Publishers, New York, USA, 1995, p.23

October 22: Robert Thurman, as for Oct. 21, p.157

October 23: Robert Thurman, as for Oct. 21, p.141

October 24: Joseph Goldstein, *The Experience of Insight*, Shambhala Publications, USA, 1976, p.59

October 25: Joseph Goldstein, as for Oct. 24, p.95

October 26: Jack Kornfield, *A Path with Heart*, Bantam Books, USA, 1993, p.226

October 27: Jack Kornfield, as for Oct. 26, p.291

October 28: Susan Moon, as for Apr. 1, p.98

October 29: Christina Feldman, *Principles of Meditation*, Thorsons, London, UK, 1998, p.33

October 30: William Hart (ed.), as for May 16, p.124

October 31: Judith Blackstone and Zoran Josipovic, as for Jan 11, p.38

November 1: P.A. Payutto, *Dependent Origination: The Buddhist Law of Conditionality*, Buddha Dhamma Foundation, Bangkok, Thailand, 1994, p.23

November 2: P.A. Payutto, as for Nov. 1, p.61

November 3: P.A. Payutto, as for Nov. 1, p.59

November 4: A.T. Ariyaratne, *Collected Works Volume 2*, Sarvodaya Research Institute, Sri Lanka, 1980, p.56

November 5: A.T. Ariyaratne, as for Nov. 4, p.21

November 6: Walpola Rahula, *What the Buddha Taught*, Grove Press, New York, USA, p.47

November 7: Walpola Rahula, as for Nov. 6, p.65

November 8: Walpola Rahula, as for Nov. 6, p.77

November 9: Kate Crosby and Andrew Skilton, *Santideva the Bodhicaryavatara*, Oxford University Press, Oxford, UK, 1995, p.59

November 10: Jack Kornfield and Paul Breiter (eds), *A Still Forest Pool: The Insight Meditation of Ajahn Chah*, The Theosophical Publishing House, IL, USA, 1985, p.55

November 11: Jack Kornfield and Paul Breiter (eds), as for Nov. 10, p.59

November 12: Ajahn Sumedho, *The Mind and the Way: Buddhist Reflections on Life*, Wisdom Publications, MA, USA, 1995, p.107

November 13: Ajahn Sumedho, as for Nov. 12, p.41

November 14: Ajahn Sumedho, as for Nov. 12, p.105

November 15: Gill Farrer-Halls, *The Illustrated Encyclopedia of Buddhist Wisdom: A Complete Introduction to the Principles and Practices of Buddhism*, Goldsfield Press Ltd, UK, 2000, p.62

November 16: Gill Farrer-Halls, as for Nov. 15, p.85

November 17: Jack Kornfield, *Living Buddhist Masters*, Unity Press, Santa Cruz, CA, USA, 1977, p.266

November 18: Jack Kornfield, as for Nov. 17, p.267

November 19: Jack Kornfield, as for Nov. 17, p.278

November 20: Ayya Khema, as for Oct. 11, p.77

November 21: Ayya Khema, as for Oct. 11, p.119

November 22: Ayya Khema, as for Oct. 11, p.88

November 23: Gill Farrer-Halls, *The World of the Dalai Lama: An Inside Look at his Life, His People and His Visitors*, Thorsons/HarperCollins Publishers, London, UK, 1998, p.64

November 24: Gill Farrer-Halls, as for Nov. 23, p.29

November 25: Renuka Singh (ed.) *The Dalai Lama's Book of Daily Meditations: The Path to Tranquillity*, Rider Books, Random House, London, UK, 1998, p.263

November 26: Aung San Suu Kyi, as for Oct. 1, p.174

November 27: Patrul Rinpoche, as for Jan 23, p.140

November 28: Timothy Freke, as for Jan 18, p.81

November 29: Judith Blackstone and Zoran Josipovic, as for Jan 11, p.115

November 30: Judith Blackstone and Zoran Josipovic, as for Jan 11, p.66

December 1: Judith Blackstone and Zoran Josipovic, as for Jan 11, p.40

December 2: Pema Chodron, as for Aug. 16, p.68

December 3: Rob Preece, *The Alchemical Buddha: Introducing the Psychology of Buddhist Tantra*, Mudra Publications, Chagford, Devon, UK, 2000, p.151

December 4: Ven. Maha Ghosananda, as for Oct. 12, p.53

December 5: Ajahn Chah, *Being Dharma: The Essence of the Buddha's Teachings*, Shambhala Publications, Boston, MA, USA, 2001, p.22

December 6: Sandy Boucher, *Opening the Lotus: A Woman's Guide to Buddhism*, Beacon Press, Boston, MA, USA, p.54

December 7: Geshe Jampa Tegcho, *Transforming the Heart: The Buddhist Way to Joy and Courage*, Snow Lion Publications, New York, USA, 1999, p.92

December 8: David Brazier, *The Feeling Buddha: An Introduction to Buddhism*, Constable Publishers, London, UK, 1997, p.83

December 9: Jim Pym, *You Don't Have to Sit on the Floor: Bringing the Insight and Tools of Buddhism into Everyday Life*, Rider Publications, London, UK, 2001, p.51

December 10: Lama Yeshe, *Introduction to Tantra: A Vision of Totality*, Wisdom Publications, Boston, MA, USA, 1987, p.42

December 11: Allan Hunt Badiner, as for Jun. 19, p.188

December 12: David Brazier, *Zen Therapy: A Buddhist Approach to Psychotherapy*, Constable Publishers, London, UK, 1995, p.107

December 13: Chogyam Trungpa, *Cutting Through Spiritual Materialism*, Shambhala Publications, Boston, USA, MA, 1973, p.98

December 14: Chogyam Trungpa, as for Dec. 13, p.83

December 15: Chogyam Trungpa, *Meditation in Action*, Shambhala Publications, Boston, MA, USA, 1991, p.45

December 16: Ayya Khema, *Bean Island: The Buddhist Practice of Inner Peace*, Wisdom Publications, USA, 1999, p.55

December 17: Chogyam Trungpa, *The Lion's Roar: An Introduction to Tantra*, Shambhala Publications, USA, 1992, p.103

December 18: Eugen Herrigel, *Zen in the Art of Archery*, Penguin Books, London, UK, 1985, p.47

December 19: Anne Bancroft, *The Pocket Buddha Reader*, Shambhala Publications, Boston, USA, 2001, p.109

December 20: Albert Low, *To Know Yourself: Talks, Stories and Articles on Zen*, Charles E. Tuttle, Boston, USA, 1997, p.19

December 21: Dr Mark Epstein, *Going to Pieces without Falling Apart: A Buddhist Perspective on Wholeness*, HarperCollins Publishers, London, UK, 1999, p.111

December 22: Edward Conze, *Buddhist Scriptures*, Penguin Books, London, UK, 1959, p.177

December 23: Chris Paulin, *Introducing Buddhism*, Windhorse Publications, Birmingham, UK, 1999, p.27

December 24: David Brazier, *The New Buddhism: A Rough Guide to a New Way of Life*, Constable Publishers, London, UK, 2001, p.178

December 25: John Wellwood, *Toward a Psychology of Awakening*, Shambhala Publications, Boston, MA, USA, 2002, p.194

December 26: Chogual Namkhai Norbu, *Dzogchen: The Self Perfected State*, Snow Lion Publications, New York, USA, 1996, p.81

December 27: Ajahn Chah, as for Dec. 5, p.69

December 28: John Wellwood, as for Dec. 25, p.17

December 29: Edward Conze (trans.), as for May 1, p.188

December 30: Edward Conze (trans.), as for May 1, p.141

December 31: Judith Blackstone and Zoran Josipovic, as for Jan 11, p.58